Warren Sumner Barlow

The Voices

Warren Sumner Barlow

The Voices

ISBN/EAN: 9783743357013

Manufactured in Europe, USA, Canada, Australia, Japa

Cover: Foto ©ninafisch / pixelio.de

Manufactured and distributed by brebook publishing software (www.brebook.com)

Warren Sumner Barlow

The Voices

THE VOICES.

("THE VOICE OF NATURE," "THE VOICE OF A PEBBLE,'
"THE VOICE OF SUPERSTITION," AND "THE
VOICE OF PRAYER.")

BY

WARREN SUMNER BARLOW.

TWELFTH EDITION.

BOSTON:
COLBY & RICH.
1888.

Entered, according to Act of Congress, in the year 1870, by
W. S. BARLOW,
In the Office of the Librarian of Congress at Washington.

TROW'S
PRINTING AND BOOKBINDING CO.,
PRINTERS AND BOOKBINDERS,
205-213 *East 12th St.*,
NEW YORK.

TO
THOSE WHO HAVE EARS
TO HEAR,
"THE VOICES" ARE RESPECTFULLY
DEDICATED.

CONTENTS.

THE VOICE OF NATURE

Is founded on the idea of
One God, with one revokeless plan,
Embracing every world and man;
That man should learn to comprehend,
That all to good results doth tend.
Page 7.

THE VOICE OF A PEBBLE

Aims to teach the Individuality of Matter and Mind,
Fraternal Charity and Love.   Page 37.

THE VOICE OF SUPERSTITION

Presents the conflict that many suppose exists between their Maker and an imaginary evil being.   Page 55.

THE VOICE OF PRAYER

Aims to inculcate the idea that
No law is suspended should earth everywhere
Unite in one chorus to swell the same prayer.
Then pray that your prayers with God's laws ever blend,
In union with *deeds* that will bless and extend;
For these are the prayers that the Lord ever heeds,
Regardless of color, of birth, or of creeds;
We thus build a ladder, each deed is a round,
Which reaches to heaven, while touching the ground.
Page 193.

VOICE OF NATURE.

PRELUDE.

ALL Nature speaks the attributes of God,
Whose vast domains of matter and of mind,
Accord forever with His holy will.
All life is an expression of His love,
All seeming death, is birth to higher life;
All discord is the fragment of a scale
Which, had man the power to comprehend,
Would be replete with harmony divine.

VOICE OF NATURE.

Eternal Father! in whose life we live,
Whose boundless love doth every blessing give,
Whose wisdom planned and beautifies the whole,
And speaks the wonders of divine control;
Whose power is ever equal to fulfill
The changeless purpose of Thy holy will;
Whose will is law, with one revokeless aim,
Through all extent eternally the same;
While Nature, loyal to her code of laws,
Responds to Thee, the Universal Cause!
From smallest atom which no eye can trace,
To suns and worlds that decorate all space,
From lowest instinct to the plane of man,
To highest seraphs, all adorn Thy plan;

Alike are objects of Thy tender care;
Alike perform their mission everywhere;
Alike adapted to the spheres they fill,
In perfect union all obey Thy will.

Relentless man! in view of truths like these,
Why sit you down in ignorance and ease?
Why falter by the road, or from it stray,
While God's eternal signals light the way?
Old honest Time—the scribe of every age—
In Nature's volume writes on every page
A universal language, understood
By every soul, that God is great and good.

From lowest stratum to the verdant plain,
Behold the links in this important chain;
Each link dependent on the one below,
Each marked with progress as we upward go;
Till vegetation spreads her carpet green,
And creeping things, and animals, are seen.
While man—the crowning apex of the whole—
Is made the temple for a living soul,

In whom all other forms and powers combine—
The union of the earthly and divine.

From grossest matter to the most refined,
Each grain is working as it was designed:
Each in its sphere their labors do impart,
Unskilled in science, and untaught by art;
Each brute fulfills its mission, small or great,
No less than kingdom formed inanimate;
Each rock a volume gilded o'er with age;
Each grain that forms it, is a written page;
Each shell contains a lesson if we seek;
Each pebbled brook with eloquence doth speak.
The rippling rill that cheers the mountain side,
Salutes its mate to form the river wide;
While arm in arm they journey to the sea,
Where all unite in joyful harmony;
Yet every breeze that fans the vacant main,
Brings back to earth the little streams again.

Lo! Spring unlocks her many frozen bands,
And melts the icy jewels from her hands;

From long repose she wakes the sleeping flowers,
Whose fragrant smiles make glad the passing hours;
Her verdant carpets all the fields adorn,
The new clad forests sparkle in the morn;
The feathered songsters tune their gladsome lay,
While genial showers and sunshine gild the day.

The changing seasons of earth's broad domains,
Bring wealth and gladness in their *daily trains;*
Thus Nature works in all her varied forms,
Through joyous sunshine, and in wint'ry storms;
While every thing in water, air, or earth,
Performs the will of Him who gave them birth:
All things co-operate, and ever blend,
To serve each other for a noble end.

Thus Nature's law directs, and all obey;
Her laws are just and have triumphant sway;

All law is love adapted to each sphere,
And thus controlled, the law is not severe;
Each has its line of life distinct to run,
All plainly marked—as plainly what to shun;
All heed God's law, can choose no other way;
This truth is clear, to act is to obey.
Can apples grow on oaks, where acorns thrive?
Can bees turn spiders and forsake their hive?
Can fishes live on trees where linnets sing?
A monkey shave his face and be a king?
Then doubt no more, for all are to fulfill
The changeless purpose of their Maker's will,
All have their proper sphere, or lot assigned,
Adapted to their nature or their mind.

While viewing thus the laws that govern these,
Beast, bird, and insect, blooming flowers and trees,
And in them all God's grand designs we trace,
We must conclude 'tis thus throughout all space;
Like the frail needle that directs afar,

If true an inch 'tis true to distant star.
Omnipotence established His decree,
Mapped out all time, no less eternity.

"Thou great First Cause" and only Cause direct,
All else existing only is *effect;*
Cause and *effect* must harmonize and blend,
To doubt the *cause,* we need but doubt the *end.*

When on the verge of Time's primeval morn,
Before a sun or satellite was born,
Or first glad ray of oriental light
Dispelled the gloom of an eternal night,
While chaos reigned through endless depths of space,
And coming years had no recording place,
Yet worlds unborn were in the womb of thought,
Which were by God and Nature long begot;
And God through LAW, by which He doth control,

Was breathing life and beauty through the
 whole;
Was working out a problem true and grand,
Which we but dimly see, less understand,
And through eternity His law reveals
His changeless plan that ignorance conceals.
Like as Himself, His law must be divine,
Through which His attributes forever shine.
God's perfect law can never be deranged;
Is ever changeless, though all else is changed:
No clause abridged, none added, none repealed;
Jehovah can not change it—*this is sealed!*
Perfection altered, would produce a flaw;
God can not *err*, hence, can not change His
 law:
While ceaseless ages constitute the past,
Though future cycles will forever last,
Unchanging law hath beautified the whole,
Outlives all ages, ever will control,
Yea, God Himself is law; and His decree
Propels the movements of eternity.

Creation but one galaxy unfurls—
Jehovah's crown a diadem of pearls!
Each star-lit gem upon the whole depends;
The whole to each, a needed influence lends:
Each orb, an aggregate of countless grains;
Each grain a key, a ponderous arch sustains;
Destroy but one, the boundless spheres will fall,
And tumble worlds to chaos, one and all;
Thus all are links in Nature's endless chain—
The hand that forged them never wrought in vain.

Great God! what wisdom is at Thy command,
What power, while worlds are balanced in Thy hand!
Thy watchful care directs the slender blade,
And warms with sunshine and protects with shade,
Enriches earth with rivers, lakes, and seas,
Directs the storm, yet whispers in the breeze,

While worlds revolve in undiscovered space,
Where weary thought can find no resting-place;
Yet not a single grain is left to chance,
Throughout creation's infinite expanse;
Thy love and wisdom mold and guide the whole,
From motes in sunbeams to all spheres that roll.

But where is man—the apex of God's love,
The link connecting earth to spheres above?
Hath he no part in this stupendous plan?
He left to grope his way as best he can?
He made to walk a dim and dangerous path,
Mid darkness, dogmas, superstition, wrath?
With feeble step, while doubts assail his mind,
A hell perhaps to shun, a heaven to find?
A hell! For whom? For man, a priest replies,
And man alone, of all beneath the skies,
Is doomed to wail in endless pain and woe,
To flaming fire, for God hath made it so,
Our Heavenly Father fired the molten lake

For His *dear children* e'er he them did make:
Thus saith the priest, and all the church believe;
Whatever he may preach, they will receive.
Who can believe, when taught by reason's light,
That man is wholly wrong, all else is right?
That God's great purpose fails with human souls,
While all of lesser value He controls!
That man alone is doomed to weep and wail,
Through endless ages in a dismal vale;
In vain to pray with supplicating cry,
" My God, how long! must I forever die?"
" Forever!" echoes from God's awful throne,
With mocks and jeers at every burdened groan![1]

O thoughtless man, reflect, can this be true,
When God who made thee, had thy end in view?
Will He who hears the ravens when they cry,

[1] Prov. i. 26.

Mock and deride thee, when no hope is nigh?
Will He who clothes the lilies of the field,
That neither toil, nor spin, nor raiment yield;
Who feeds the fowls that never reap nor sow,
Extends His watchful care where'er they go;
Will He who clothes the grass which is to-day,
While all its beauty quickly fades away,
Forget His image—His immortal child?[1]
Is he alone derided and defiled?
Or left to tread the downward thoroughfare,
With Satan to bewilder and ensnare,
And urge him on to death and dark despair?
"O ye of little faith!" let *reason sway:*
Are not your souls more precious far than they?

Believe that God thy Father is thy friend,
And hath designed thee for a noble end:
Made earth thy home, selected each his clime,
The age in which to live, and length of time;
Ordained the path for every human soul,

[1] Matt. vi. 26–30.

Before it had a thought of self-control:
Illumines each with Hope's inspiring ray,
And gives a foretaste of immortal day;
While all are molded by the hand of fate,
Before the mind attains its conscious state:
"Just as the twig is bent the tree's inclined,"
Is no less truthful of the human mind.

Doth man select his native land? his birth?
Can any these *reject*, throughout the earth?
Yet clime and birth direct and mold the mind,
And mark the path to which man is inclined.

Who gave the different faiths their hope and fear?
And each the Bible they so much revere?
All claiming leaders from the upper sphere,
Divinely sent to banish every tear.

The Hindoo reads with reverence the Shaster;
The Persian takes his law from Zoroaster;

Mohammed wrote the Koran as inspired:
All are revered as if by heaven required.
While thus *sincere*, the law to each is right;
Each page and volume beams with heavenly
    light.
Who made us Christians and gave us our law?
All *others wrong*, but *ours without a flaw?*
Are thus nine-tenths of all mankind deceived
In their religion, honestly believed?
Is God thus partial to the human race?
While love divine is seen in all we trace?
While suns and systems move in order grand,
Propelled by laws ordained by His command;
While every grain in this terrestrial ball,
Alike sustains, yet each sustaining all;
While all creation is but one design,
Through which eternal harmonies combine,
Who will presume, in this stupendous plan,
That He who governs all, neglected man?
That He directs revolving worlds with care,
Yet lays for man a fatal, artful snare?

That God hath made immortal souls in vain,
Or, what is worse, made most for endless pain!
That His dear children under any sky,
Were made immortal to forever die?
Or that there can exist a human soul,
Devoid of God's divine, supreme control?
For He adapts the food to every mind,
And shapes the destiny of all mankind.
Thus every people hath a form of praise,
Most wisely suited to its wants and ways;
And every soul in this and every land,
Is kindly nurtured by a Father's hand;
And is directed by unchanging law,
To choose the right, from danger to withdraw.

While worlds by kind attraction heed their way,
They also firm repellant force obey;
And move and shine while endless ages roll,
Propelled by laws that ever will control.
And mind no less than matter will obey,
Though oft it may transgress and long delay.

The pains of sin are friends in timely need,
To teach mankind their evil ways to heed;
While peace that flows from actions well defined,
Will guide our footsteps and direct the mind;
And as we each obey or violate,
We learn to love the right, the wrong to hate·
Thus are we taught by every word and deed,
To shun the paths of sin, God's laws to heed.

Why not to rocky height and brink repair,
And make a fatal leap, devoid of care?
Why not descend Niagara's awful roar,
Or in a frail balloon the stars explore?
Why not plunge headlong into raging fire?
Or when you thirst, a boiling fount desire?
Why not on thorny pillows rest your head?
And with hot embers make your nightly bed?
Because unchanging law, without delay,
In *love* chastises when we disobey,
To teach us all the true and better way.

Why not, when howling storms their fury
    pour,
Expel the freezing traveller from your door?
Why happy when he eats his cheerful meal,
And blesses God you have a heart to feel?
Because the law of love is ever sure
To bless each soul who kindly feeds the poor.
How wise this law, how powerful for good,
When once obeyed, and fully understood.
How true that pain, with all its varied ills,
And every pleasure that our being thrills,
Are each effects of their producing cause,
Sustained by God's divine unchanging laws.
False steps reveal the alphabet of truth,
Though sad the lesson to a wayward youth;
If age or youth from Nature's laws depart
Like children burned, they learn to dread the
    smart;
Eternal justice poises every deed,
With joy, or sorrow, as we sow the seed.
Thus retribution comes with kindly pain,

To teach transgressors not to stray again.
And holy joys will never be delayed,
When laws are known, and rigidly obeyed.
Thus all by mingled pleasures, pains, and fears,
Will learn the way as they advance in years.

That God ordained the whole is understood
To ultimate in universal good;
Yet hath no less decreed that man shall be,
Within a *given sphere*, an agent free ;
As fishes well secured in globes of glass,
Are free within, though none without can pass;
While they, like us, look outward all around,
May often wish a larger range was found.
But highest wisdom hath ordained this plan,
To focalize the feeble powers of man;
Where each may freely choose a field of
    thought—
May grope in darkness, or be wisely taught;
Where all *will* learn, as laws are understood,
To harmonize with universal good.

Thus God ordained that every wayward soul,
Should walk in wisdom's ways by *self-control.*
Hence man's free agency is not denied,
While God's grand purposes are glorified.

Why then repine? why not pursue the goal?
Obey the high emotions of the soul?
They are the voice of God in tones of love,
Inviting each to joys that are above.
Our aspirations ever upward soar;
We never hope for less, but always more.
And can the Author of our hopes decry
And leave a famished soul to starve and die?
O God, forbid! our longing nature cries,
While hope confiding mounts the azure skies.
Sweet hope! thou beacon-light to weary souls,
Illumed by Him who everywhere controls,
A cheerful promise, full of holy joy,
A glimpse, a touch, that time can not destroy;
And he who doubts, must question means and ends,
And think that God is *bankrupt and suspends!*

A glorious future cheers the human race;
Unending Progress hath no resting-place;
While all our fondest hopes exultant rise,
To reach the land where sorrow only dies;
To meet our happy friends who went before,
Who'll gladly greet us as we near the shore.

Let stoics misconstrue Divine decrees,
Usurp the rule, give heaven to whom they please,
'Tis yet their mission, and no doubt it's best,
That they should belch the fire that burns their breast.
They fain believe the Lord doth oft repent,[1]
In sorrow walks, in sadness doth relent,
Consults with man who arbitrates his cause;
Is oft induced to compromise His laws;
That Satan thwarted God with mother Eve,
Which made the Lord repent and deeply grieve

[1] Gen vi. 6; Ex. xxxii. 14; 1 Saml. xv. 35.

If man doth not comport with God's decree,
Or runs a race that God did not foresee,
Or if He saw, not choosing to prevent,
Or, choosing, had not power omnipotent;
Or, having power, had not the traits combined,
To mold and fashion man to suit His mind,
Then may old orthodoxy well repose,
Upon its gloomy doctrines and its woes.

Child of thy Father God, use common sense—
Stand forth a man,—believe Omnipotence!
Think for thyself, maintain thy high behest;
Be happy now, yea, evermore be blest;
O thou desponding soul, no longer grieve,
For more than thou canst hope, thou wilt receive;
Ne'er doubt though seeming discord grates thine ear,
Though disappointed hope brings sorrow's tear,
Though man assail his brother man with hate,
And wars and famine seem to be thy fate;
Wait the result: these scenes are but a part,

Like shadows on a landscape rich with art;
All move in concert under wise control;
No part is evil could we view the whole.

Shall we illustrate this important truth,
And introduce a country while in youth?
Then, in its native state, a prairie view,
Whose waving grass the plow will soon
    subdue;
Its rolling surface far exceeds our gaze,
Where herds run wild and wander while they
    graze:
Where unmolested Nature is at ease,
And flowers amid tall grasses kiss the breeze.
The nimble deer with undiverted bound,
Fears not the hunter, or the hunter's hound;
The prairie wolf his bleeding prey devours,
Howls undisturbed through all the nightly
    hours;
The busy ant her humble home erects,
From heat and cold it shelters and protects.

Contented Nature marks her yearly rounds,
No hand of art intrudes upon her grounds.

But what comes here (these lower tribes
    demand),
That brings but death and darkness in its hand!
Usurps the rule, upturns the living sod,
Entombs fair Nature's face beneath the clod?
Blights all our hopes, destroys our floral home,
While sure destruction is our fearful doom!
A fatal scourge to every living thing,
A horrid monster, though he must be king!

Thus all of these unite with solemn vow,
Against the quiet farmer with his plow;
The grand results and blessings which will
    blend,
They can not see, much less can comprehend.
But shining grain will soon the farmer greet,
With golden corn and waving fields of wheat;
The humble cot will mark his happy home

Upon the spot where howling wolves did roam;
The village bells respond from hill to plain,
And join in chorus to the distant main.
Thus cities, towns, and nations will have sway,
And plant their footsteps where these tribes decay.
This is established law by wise decree,
And countless blessings in the whole we see.

Take courage, then, O man! when doubts arise,
And clouds and darkness intercept your skies;
Be not like thoughtless tribes, or senseless minds,
Who know no God, much less His wise designs.
Believe that from the blood of *martyrs* slain,
More perfect fruit will bless the earth again;
That pain and evil are but friends disguised,
That tears will all be jewels crystallized.
Why should we question Him who ruleth all

Presides with care though empires rise and fall!
As cycles move successively around,
God's love and wisdom will in all be found.
An age with God is but one pendulum stroke,
Which worlds and systems in their rounds
    provoke;
While mortal man, with feeble fleeting breath,
Scarce views an inch of time before his death.
In vain he strives to learn when Time began;
The more he learns, the less he feels a man.
Yet ages roll their centuries behind,
An undisputed record of God's mind:
Eternal ages but His plan reveals,
While fleeting time all but a glimpse conceals;
We scarcely reach in wisdom letter A,
While cumbered with this tenement of clay,
Much less a sentence can we comprehend,
Of vast eternity that hath no end!

Who with one letter can decide a name,
While saint and sinner each begin the same!

Or with a sentence never understood,
Who will presume to arbitrate with God?
Yet with one ray of feeble, doubtful light,
Presumptuous man would rule the Infinite!
But coming ages will to all unfold
The wisdom that no mortal tongue hath told
This life is but a rudimental sphere,
We barely learn our ignorance while here;
Yet Hope is born with unattained desires,
And to immortal life each soul aspires.
In this important truth all tongues agree,
That man was made for immortality.
Death kindly comes and opens wide the door,
And lights our passage to the golden shore;
Oblivion spans the gulf while on we tread
The silent pathway of the living dead.
Then let earth join with aspirations high,
Proclaim this glorious truth—WE NEVER DIE!
The fields of thought that baffle modern lore,
We in our march of progress will explore;
The highest aspirations of each soul

Will more than be attained as ages roll;
The stellar worlds of beauty, all so grand,
Will be our walks of pleasure at command.
We'll leave behind the distant orbs of light,
Like stepping-stones, as we pursue our flight;
We'll pat the Bear and Tiger passing up,
And use the Northern Dipper as a cup;
Then strike the trail where shining comets play,
O'er trackless paths along the Milky Way.
We then can learn of God among the spheres,
And feel the folly of our early years;
The orient fields of lucid amber light
Will cheer us on and on amid our flight;
New beauties in concentric circles rise,
Will span the endless arches of the skies.
Amid these rapturous scenes we'll hie to earth,
To childhood's home—the land that gave us
  birth.
Our friends who yet remain will need our care,
While they a little longer linger there;
We'll prove that we yet live, and love them still,

And though unseen, kind offices fulfill;
Can raise their souls from earth to joys above;
Can sweeten daily toil with peace and love;
Can elevate the poor desponding soul,
Who from surroundings hath no self-control;
Can visit prisons, where our brothers dwell,
And cheer the lonely, gloomy, darkened cell;
Dispel the tears of sorrow, banish pain,
And prove to man that he will live again.
Oh yes! we'll come the human race to cheer,
Wherever earth is watered by a tear.
The mother comes to bless her infant boy,
To guard the tender bud with holy joy:
Her love so pure on earth is not defiled,
But with a mother's love, she loves her child.
And children seized by Death's relentless hand
Oft gladly mingle in the broken band.
The brittle thread of life can not divide,
For angel friends are often by your side;
Thus heaven and earth are joined in happy twain,
And in this glorious union will remain.

How wise, how great, how wonderful the plan!
A boundless field for undeveloped man!
God's works and ways we ne'er can compre-
    hend,
CREATION, this one theme may never end;
His omnipresence, love, and wise control,
Are each immortal themes for every soul.
Then let all nations join in chorus grand,
Proclaim the tidings far o'er sea and land;
Let worlds on worlds reiterate the song,
That God our Father NEVER DOETH WRONG!
As He alone is infinite in power,
Desire is action, now and evermore;
As wisdom shines omnipotently grand,
'Tis traced through all the workings of His
    hand:
As God is love, all things are lovely too,
And rightly seen, His love in all we view;
While Nature's countless voices all proclaim.
Eternal progress is the end and aim.

VOICE OF A PEBBLE.

PRELUDE.

Throughout the realm of matter and of mind,
Variety in countless forms we find;
Yet all creation is but one grand thought,
Which God in love and wisdom hath outwrought;
Hence all are *one, to God,* and one is *all;*
Each part a fragment fitted to the line,
To which no accident can e'er befall,
But in God's temple will forever shine.

VOICE OF A PEBBLE.

A PEBBLE in my hand I hold,
  From yonder limpid brook,
And read its lessons manifold,
  As one might read a book.

It says, Throughout this wondrous sphere,
  Where'er our thoughts may bound,
To distant worlds, though far or near,
  No one like me is found.

I am myself, will ever be,
  And can not be another:
My sphere is fixed eternally,
  And Nature is my brother.

While this great truth relates to me,
  A part is only told;

For every thing in land or sea,
    Is cast in diff'rent mold.

The pebbles round the ocean deep,
    Which every wave doth wear,
The shining leaves the seasons keep,
    No two alike are there.

Of all the grains composing earth,
    And vegetation fair,
All forms of life of every birth,
    In water, earth, or air,

The rule holds good, no two are found
    Whose pattern is the same;
And could we trace creation round,
    We would this truth proclaim.

The forms of life that meet the eye,
    Wherever we may gaze,
With varied robes from Nature's dye,
    In every form and phase,

Are but the outward signs that mark
   Their features to the world,
Their nature yet is in the dark,
   Their motives not unfurled.

Some kick, some bite, some lick your hands,
   And some will prance and play,
Some meekly bow at your commands,
   While others flee away.

Some climb the trees, some bore the ground,
   Some gnash their teeth and growl;
Some only through the day are found,
   All night some whoop and howl.

All must reveal the pent-up fires
   Of animated force,
Portraying ever God's desires,
   From which there's no divorce.

Thus Ætna heaves his foaming crest,
   And belches fire and smoke;

Expels the moaning of his breast,
    The obstacles that choke,

And gains relief and acts his part,
    Like waves that beat the shore;
Or throbbings in the lion's heart,
    That stimulate his roar.

A chain of varied links we see
    Wherever God is found:
If two alike will ever be,
    Infinitude is bound.

In earth, in air, in sea, or space,
    Through worlds and suns that roll,
A God in endless forms we trace,
    Whose wisdom guides the whole.

Jehovah speaks in all we see,
    Whose countless tongues rehearse
Harmonious strains of melody,
    Throughout the universe.

All have their proper spheres to fill,
    With settled rule in view;
Each must perform its Maker's will,
    With *nothing else to do.*

The waters from the distant hill,
    Or cascade in the lawn,
The mighty river or the rill,
    All to the ocean borne,

No more to Nature's path incline,
    Or follow God's decree,
No more fulfill His wise design,
    Than every thing we see.

No hand can injure or deface
    One particle or grain;
Each occupies and fills the place
    That wisdom did ordain.

As well assail the storms that blow,
    Or proud Niag'ra's roar,

Or ocean tides that come and go,
    Or waves that lash the shore,

Or blazing comets in their flight,
    Or worlds that roll on high,
Or dim the shining orbs of light,
    Or God himself defy;

For all obey with cheerful zeal
    The mandate God hath given;
And each alike His laws reveal,
    Throughout the vault of heaven.

All worlds have their appointed spheres,
    Distinctively their own;
Their length of days and rolling years;
    Their longitude and zone.

Could aught suspend these potent laws,
    This equipoise of power,
And intercept the Great First Cause,
    But for a single hour;

Should but one star impede its flight,
    Or lose its time and place,
Or seek another's trail of light
    Throughout the realms of space,

Death's dark convulsive waves would lash,
    Creation's boundless shore,
And worlds with universal crash
    Would sink to rise no more.

Thus Nature, with united voice,
    Proclaims its Maker's praise;
Though laws propel, it seems of choice,
    That every thing obeys.

If then whate'er on earth appears,
    With all that moves above,
Combine like music of the spheres,
    To prove eternal love,

How is it with created man,
    The image of his God,

Who though his life is but a span,
   Doth rule this earthly clod?

His form is comely and erect,
   With features fair and fine,
No sculptor can a fault detect,
   Or criticise a line.

His noble frame out-rivals art,
   By ligaments entwined;
While membranes, muscles, all impart
   Their form and strength combined.

His life-blood currents ebb and flow,
   The airy tissues greet,
And leave their burden to and fro
   At each successive beat.

The brain, with all its countless nerves,
   On guard by night and day—
With constant vigilance observes,
   Reports without delay.

The eye, the window of the soul,
    On earth and heaven doth gaze,
The ear sweet melodies control,
    And tongue that speaks God's praise.

The countless wonders of this frame,
    (A portion only told,
Ten thousand parts, no two the same,)
    Their uses do unfold.

But each adapted to its place,
    In harmony all blend,
A perfect union here we trace;
    The parts do not contend:

For all unite with one accord.
    To form and fashion man—
The image of his maker, Lord,
    In wisdom of His plan.

Yet no two men alike are found,
    In body or in mind,

And those who view the world around,
    This truth will ever find.

For each sustains a separate part,
    To an important whole;
Each fills his place and does impart
    The motives of his soul.

Each has a mission of his own,
    Adapted to his skill,
To be sustained by him alone;
    Which no one else can fill.

No two alike are wise and great,
    No two alike can see,
And those who would but imitate,
    Make war on God's decree.

Variety marks every deed,
    And modifies the whole,
Imparts to each an honest creed,
    Adapted to the soul.

Gives occupation to the mind,
   On every plane of thought;
Each in his sphere will pleasure find,
   There only should be sought.

Some love to plow the trackless seas,
   Some in the workshop toil,
Some fain would fly against the breeze,
   While others till the soil.

Some love to delve in musty lore,
   Some live by what they say,
While others would the world explore,
   And gladly lead the way.

And though ten thousand may pursue
   The self-same occupation,
No two alike the same will do
   In any land or nation.

But each adapted to his place,
   The world moves gladly on;

Each for himself, yet by the race
　　Is ever moved upon.

Each is a unit, though a link
　　In an unending chain,
Yet for himself should ever think,
　　And self-hood thus maintain.

To each a birthright is decreed,
　　That shapes our aim and end,
Secured and vested in a deed,
　　That all should well defend.

Oh, then retain thy rightful sway
　　Of that which is thine own;
Remember Esau gave away
　　His birthright for a bone.

A creed is written on each breast,
　　That God will justify;
Let each maintain his high behest,
　　Though all the world decry.

When priests and parsons crowd your path,
    With hell beset your way,
And preach that God is full of wrath,
    Because you're not as they,

They little think that God hath made
    Unlike ten thousand flowers,
And giveth each the sun and shade,
    And genial, gentle showers;

Each flower ordained itself to be,
    None other to desire,
A type of nature's harmony,
    That angels must admire.

Should roses in their rich attire,
    More humble flowers disdain?
Or in a warlike mood require
    All other rivals slain?

Should creeping vines that hug the earth,
    Assail the morning glory,

Because of their more lowly birth,
  Who could believe the story?

Each hath its mission everywhere,
  And all obey God's will,
By being *most* of what they are,
  And thus their end fulfill.

Then let each soul with all its powers,
  Forever seek to be
As perfect in itself as flowers,
  Type of Divinity.

And as our feeble minds unfold,
  We children of the sod,
In every object may behold
  The alphabet of God.

Then let us deal with charity,
  Be hopeful, not bewail,
Each glimpse of truth a rarity,
  Will finally prevail.

For who can doubt that motives good,
  May govern every mind?
For it is plainly understood,
  That God to all is kind.

All in their sphere fulfill their task,
  As roars volcanic fire;
The good to follow will unmask,
  When evil deeds expire.

All then fulfill a wise design,
  Though devious seems the way;
While all in harmony combine,
  And each and all obey.

With God thy Father, man thy brother
  Oh, be thyself a man,
Each for himself, yet for each other,
  Is Heav'ns eternal plan.

VOICE OF SUPERSTITION

PRELUDE.

Who can believe that God hath ever changed,
Or that His holy plans have been deranged?
Yet creeds have so dethroned our *common sense*—
Our just conceptions of Omnipotence—
So slandered reason and God's light within,
To doubt that God *repents*, is wilful sin!
Within the Bible, much I love, and bless,
I might love *more*, if God I could love *less;*
But when I read that God's great plans have failed—
That He repents when Satan's power prevailed—
That Satan ruled from Eden to the cross,
Though finding gold, all *this* is empty dross!
O man, be just, be true to reason's light,
Defend and cherish all that seemeth right,
No longer bow to priest's delusive nod,
But vindicate the attributes of God.

VOICE OF SUPERSTITION.

It hath been said, in ages long since gone,
When Time was young, or in its early dawn,
That from chaotic matter God designed
This little world, to represent His mind.
But as all Nature was an endless night,[1]
His first commandment was "Let there be light!
When, from eternal darkness light was born,
Which ushered in the grand primeval morn.
Thus darkness fled before the verge of day,
And hid itself beyond the shady way.
The waters next divided from the land,
While vegetation came at His command.
When fragrant flowers and fruitful trees un
    furled,
The Lord was pleased that He had made a world

[1] Gen. i. 3.

Three days and nights disclosed their light and
    shade,[1]
Before the sun, or moon, or stars were made!
Upon the fourth, the golden sun was born,[2]
To rule the day and gild the early morn;
The moon and stars to shed their silver light,
And cheer the silent hours of tranquil night.
At length, all forms of life in wondrous train,
And man, the monarch of the land and main,
'Mid Eden's flowers and fruits in beauty stood,
While God, delighted, said that all was good.[3]
Thus heaven and earth reveal His works and
    ways,
And show a work completed in six days.

And while He sought refreshing slumber sweet,
Amid the arches of His grand retreat,
He little dreamed that other powers would rise,
That seraphs who inhabited the skies,

---

[1] Gen. i. 13.—[2] i. 14–18.—[3] i. 20–31 - ii. 2.

Would envy Him His power and glorious plan,
And wage a warfare and bewilder man.
Yet sad to tell, the angel host rebelled,
And in the contest were from heaven expelled.
Thus dawned the days of darkness, death, and evil,
And introduced the serpent called the devil,[1]
Who, now on hostile terms with God of all,
With fell intent resolved that man should fall,
At once proceeds to Eden's calm retreat,
With plans matured, God's purpose to defeat;
In serpent form upon his tail he walked,
With forked tongue he eloquently talked,
And thus addressed the happy EDEN pair:—
"Why not partake of every tree so fair?"
"We will, save one, but that we must deny,
God said, 'the day ye eat thereof ye die.'"[2]

"Ye shall *not* die! I pray you have no fear,
You'll see with open eyes and vision clear,

---

[1] Rev. xii. 7, 8, 9.—[2] Gen. ii. 17.

And be like gods, well knowing good and evil.
God knows 'tis true, though spoken by the
   devil."[1]

He gave the fruit to Eve while thus he spake,
Who acquiescing gladly did partake:
And willing with her husband to divide,
Persuaded him to share it with his bride.

Thus dowered with visions of immortal youth,
They found that Satan had but uttered truth.[2]

God being rested by His late repose,[3]
At cool of day into the garden goes;
And not perceiving them, His charming pair,
His voice "walked" forth upon the balmy air,
And circled round among fair Eden's bowers,
'Till died its echoes 'mid the fragrant flowers
In search of Adam, whom He did not see,
Because he *hid from God behind a tree;*[4]

[1] Gen. iii. 4, 5, 22.—[2] Gen. iii. 7.—[3] Ex. xxxi. 17.—[4] Gen. iii. 8.

But when espied, the truth did not conceal,
For frankly did they each the fact reveal.

When God had *learned* what Satan had been
    doing—
That Eve and Adam, knowledge were pursu-
    ing,
Incensed on them his fearful wrath he hurled.
And for their disobedience, cursed the world;
Condemned His holy pair, proclaimed their fall—
And thus pronounced his sentence upon all:

Now Satan (being on the *docket* first),
"Above all beasts and cattle art thou cursed,
Upon thy belly shalt thou wend thy ways,
And live on dust the remnant of thy days:
Hate for thy seed, the woman's seed shall feel,
And bruise thy head, and thou shalt bruise
    his heel;'[1]

[1] Gen. iii. 14, 15.

And thou, O woman! for this wicked deed,
In pain and sorrow multiply thy seed;
And to thy husband thy desire shall be,
Submissive thou, he shall rule over thee.[1]

Now Adam, as it was thy wicked choice,
To listen to the tones of woman's voice,
And didst with her forbidden fruit partake,
The earth is ever curséd for thy sake;
In sweat and sorrow eat thy daily bread,
With thorns and thistles in thy path to tread."[2]

Thus were they banished from their Eden home,
With Satan in a barren world to roam;
And lost the title to their first estate;
God set the trap, and well arranged the bait,
That Satan might prevail and seal the fate
Of all the race of man for what they ate;

[1] Gen. iii. 16.—[2] iii. 17, 18, 19.

Because they had a thirst for truth and knowledge,
And had no other chance to go to college:
Thus like the gods, they learned the good and evil,
But for this knowledge they might thank the devil.

And now from their approach to guard the tree,
Whose fruit to taste is immortality,
A sword of flame, still turning every way,
Flashes from hand cherubic, night and day.[2]

INTERLUDE.

(If God designed that man should *not* rebel,
Not eat forbidden fruit and go to hell,
Why did He not defend the *fatal* tree,
And thus protect the race eternally?
But no! the record hath most plainly told,
The fruit was good, and pleasant to behold;
The tree to be desired to make one wise,
With Satan left to counsel and advise.
With access free from every side around,
Within their reach the charming fruit was found;

[1] Gen. iii. 22.—[2] iii. 22, 23, 24.

Its fragrant odor mingled with their breath,
While all conspired to urge them on to death.
Oh, why was man in this dread hour neglected,
And left alone with Satan, unprotected?
To bring a damning curse upon his head,
And sound the awful dirge—THE RACE IS DEAD!
Or did God *choose* that Adam and his wife,
Should eat of *this*, but *not* the tree of life?
The record this opinion justifies,
And only he who blindly reads, denies;
For all conspired with charming fruit so sweet,
To urge them to the fatal tree and eat;
While flaming swords repelled the fated pair,
Forever from the tree of life so fair.)

Yet Adam knew, and fondly loved his wife,[1]
But now begins their sad career of life.
Eve bore a son, named Cain, to till the ground,
And Abel next, who did in flocks abound;
Their wants by daily toil were well supplied,
Had all they needed, yea, and more beside;
From which they made their offerings to the Lord
The choicest products which they could afford.

[1] Gen. iv. 1, 2.

God only pleased with Abel's, strange to tell;[1]
Filled Cain with anger and his features fell.
God thus respecting one, and not the other,
A quarrel rose, in which Cain slew his brother
For this offense the Lord in vengeance raved,
And cursed His child that kindness might have
    saved

Cain now forsook his farm and fled from God,[2]
Eastward of Eden, in the land of Nod.
While thus remote from God in foreign land,
Who there should greet him, and extend her
    hand,
But charming woman, in his state forlorn,
Before a daughter *ever had been born.*
While cursed of God, and doomed to separa-
    tion,
He then to woman looked for consolation;
She bore and blessed him with a charming son;
And now the race of Cain was well begun.

[1] Gen. iv. 4, 5, 11.—[2] iv. 16

Cain built a city, Enoch was its name,[1]
His eldest son was also called the same
And now it came to pass upon the earth,[2]
That sons and daughters were of frequent birth,
That generations then were multiplied,
And in their growing strength the Lord defied
While God beheld the wickedness of earth,
That evil only followed every birth,
Grieved to His heart, repented making man,[3]
Because the devil foiled Him in His plan.
This unforeseen defeat, and sad condition,
In its reaction roused the Lord's ambition,
Who now resolved that man and beast should die,
With creeping things, and birds that cleave the sky,
For "it repented Him He made them all,"
And every tribe of life alike must fall,[4]
Excepting only those the ark up bore,
And righteous family of good old Noah,

[1] Gen. iv. 17.—[2] vi. 1.—[3] vi. 5, 6.—[4] vi. 7.

Who built the ark tempestuous seas to ride,
In which he took all flesh and food beside.

INTERLUDE.

(The folly of this story is quite clear,
As all these tribes were fed at least a year,
Within a space not half their cubic feet,
While most of them *ten times* their bulk would eat.)

Now came the mighty flood with waters deep,
Its rolling waves o'er mountain tops did sweep;
Nor cries for help, nor prayers that Heaven assail
With earnest pleas for mercy, could avail;
No hill was left to echo, nor to save
The dying victims from a watery grave;
All topmost peaks were sought, yet seen no more,
A boundless ocean raged without a shore;
All life was hushed on earth God made so fair,
The mournful billows sighed in sadness there,

And howling tempests rocked the world to sleep,
Amid the surges of the rolling deep,
And closed a world-wide grave with none to weep.[1]

INTERLUDE.

(Hard to relate, yet harder understood,
Why all was evil, God created good;
Why such a fate should now befall mankind,
When all for good their Maker had designed;
That evil uncreated should prevail,
And with success the powers of truth assail;
That God's great plan should now forever fall,
And hell with death and devils get us all;
That Satan and his host alone should live,
Yet run at large permitted to deceive.
If Satan *caused* all evil to prevail,
Why did not God the *cause* at once assail?
What lasting good can any one expect,
While cause *remains*, by punishing effect?
Be as it may, the devil gained his plan,
God made his title good by drowning man

[1] Gen. vi. & vii.

Thus Nature wept in sadness o'er the tomb,
That draped the earth in universal gloom.
One righteous family alone reserved,
With this the race of man must be preserved;
Which being just, the right would only do,
Like as at first, God now begins anew.)

The waters on the earth twelve months remained,
But where they *went*, this knowledge none have gained.
We only learn the waters were abated,
For this is all that Moses has related;
The vessel rested on a mountain side,
And in due time the face of Nature dried;
Then God to Noah in his ark thus spake,
"Go forth, and with thee every creature take."
Noah obeyed, and then an altar built,
Where blood of all clean beasts and fowls was spilt,
And on the altar rose their burning flavor,
Which to the Lord was a sweet smelling savor.[1]

[1] Gen. viii.

Pleased with Noah, the Lord in kindness
spake:
"The ground no more is cursed for thy sake;
As I have done I will not do again;
While earth exists its beauty shall remain;
Seed time and harvest, cold and heat not cease;
Receive my blessing, and your race increase;
My everlasting covenant is sealed,
And token of remembrance is revealed,
My bow within the clouds the earth will span,
That I may not forget my pledge to man."[1]

This righteous man began to till the soil,
A fruitful vineyard blessed his early toil;
Its juice was sweet, and pleasant to his taste,
Of which he freely drank with too much haste;
So freely he imbibed until at length,
He fell deprived of reason and of strength.

Thus fell the second Adam, like the first,

[1] Gen. ix. 9-17

VOICE OF SUPERSTITION.

Let him who reads be judge which was the worst.
But this you will perceive, without much thinking,
The first by eating fell, the last by drinking.
The first at once his nakedness concealed,
While Noah's shame was ruefully revealed,
Who cursed his grandson while a verdant youth,
Because his father saw the *naked truth;*[1]
And he of all the earth God chose to save,
Was now prepared to fill a drunkard's grave.
Thus far the devil every time succeeded,
At least in getting all the Lord most needed

INTERLUDE.

(We would not notice this disgusting tale.
Did not believers of its truth prevail;
Whose many sects are scattered far and wide
Through every land across the ocean tide.

[1] Gen. ix 20-25

To every tongue these errors would be sent,
And for this purpose gold is freely spent,
To shackle reason, and debase the soul,
By loving God whom Satan does control.
And men who seem quite honest and sincere,
Yet preach these errors and this God revere;
Disrobe the great First Cause, all just and wise,
And make a God that Reason must despise,
Possessing all the lower traits of man,
Without the power to execute His plan;
A tripartition Godhead all in one,
Where Father is not older than his Son.
That Father, Son, and yet the Holy Ghost,
Are three, yet one, who rule the heavenly host,
To combat sin, and extricate mankind,
And yet with Satan most are left behind.
Oh, would that it were true that this was all,
That only man corrupted had a fall!
But oh, how sad, while we the page pursue
(Yet doubly sad to those who think it true),
That God is made to foster sin and shame,
And be the willing author of the same.[1]
Read, pause, and ponder on the subject well,
All preconceived ideas at once expel,
Receive with candor that which seemeth right,
And thus reject all evil with delight;

[1] Isaiah xlv. 7.; Rom. ix. 18.

While thus untrammeled and with heart sincere,
Let judgment dictate and you need not fear.

You now can say that God is good and wise;
Sustains and rules all worlds within the skies·
Created man a noble end to fill;
That worlds and man reflect His holy will;
That every thing on earth, in sea, or air,
Alike are objects of His tender care;
That nothing made was ever made in vain,
And all that is, His wisdom did ordain;
That one stupendous plan pervades the whole;
That God is love, and has supreme control—
Our Heavenly Father whom we should not fear,
A God whom men and angels must revere.

But we will find, as we peruse the page,
The God portrayed is oft a God of rage,[1]
That He doth govern as frail men entreat,[2]
And what He wills some other powers defeat,[3]
That He with willing hands brings death and pain,
Whose vengeance feeds and feasts upon the slain;[4]
That when a battle raged, to suit His will,
He made the orbs of day and night stand still;

---

[1] Heb. iii. 11.—[2] Ex. xxxii. 1-14; John xi. 22.—[3] Ezek. xxxiii. 11.—[4] Ex. xii. 29.

Thus to protract the bloody scene at night,
He gladly volunteers to hold the light;
And intercepts revolving worlds on high,
That He may see His children fight and die!

And when He heard the cry, or wail of sorrow,
Come up to Him from Sodom and Gomorrah,
Could not conjecture what it was about,
As His remote location made Him doubt.
(To Sodom and Gomorrah I will go,
And when I *learn* what they have done, I'll know;
Thus saith the page, as all can see and read;[1]
But light and truth these sayings will not heed.)
With what He heard, not being well delighted,
Came down to see, He being quite near-sighted;
Thus saw, and learned what He knew not before,
Which to His knowledge added one thing more.
Who can revere and love a God like this,
And trust their souls with Him for happiness!
'Tis not the God who everywhere resides,
And with omniscience over all presides,
Whose life pervades all Nature everywhere;
Whose love and wisdom all His creatures share;
Who over Nature holds eternal sway,
And worlds and suns revolve while they obey;

---

[1] Gen. xviii. 20 21.

VOICE OF SUPERSTITION.

Who lives in matter gross, and most refined,
Controls the whole, and fashions every mind.)

But to proceed (yet please excuse digression,
When thoughts intrude and urge a brief ex-
    pression).
Next Abraham was chosen to express,
Jehovah's holy will and righteousness,
That every people should confess His sway,
And gladly learn His precepts to obey.[1]

But how could God to lofty hopes aspire,
While now His chosen leader was a liar?[2]
And by this deed, was made an heir of hell,
Where liars all eternally must dwell?[3]
Thus forced from Satan to procure His seed,
His hope for righteous fruit was poor indeed,
And yet the Lord, by his intrusive will,
Revoked what He intended to fulfill;
And as the record stands we must conclude
That Abraham had reason to intrude;

[1] Gen. xxii.—[2] xii.—[3] Rev. xxi. 8.

Behold when threat'ning storms of fearful rage,
Reflect God's purpose on the sacred page,
The patriarch plead with mingled pain and sorrow,
That He would spare old Sodom and Gomorrah;
Again, and yet again, he urged their cause,
Entreating Him to modify His laws;
Impelled by love, while hope inspired his soul,
He plead with God, His anger to control;
With "peradventure" molding every strain,
Without this pond'rous word all hope was vain
Of safety for the cities of the plain.
And thus he prayed, that wives and daughters fair
Might not with wicked men His vengeance share.

God, being moved with his benignant plea,
Was half inclined with Abra'm to agree;
At once proposed to compromise His plan,
Change His design and pity fallen man;

And said, "If fifty righteous men are found,
I'll spare the cities and the land around."[1]
But "peradventure" ringing in His ear,
His love awakened for His children dear,
He now would save them all for forty-five,[2]
Protect their homes, and families alive.
For forty, then for thirty did he plead,[3]
Until the Lord again with him agreed;
With "peradventure" next he plead for twenty,
And God at once agreed that that was plenty.[4]
"Oh, don't be angry, Lord! do save for ten,
'Tis my last plea:" to which God said, Amen![5]
But as the righteous ten could not be found,
Destruction came and circled them around.

INTERLUDE.

(Oh, why did Abram cease their cause to plead,
When God with him so willingly agreed!
One "peradventure" more had quenched the fires
One righteous man had answered His desires.

[1] Gen. xviii. 24.—[2] xviii. 28.—[3] xviii. 29, 30.—[4] xviii. 31.—
[5] xviii. 32.

But sad the fate of Sodom and Gomorrah,
A fiery deluge filled the land with sorrow;
God's flaming vengeance thirsting for the slaughter,
Rained showers of fire from heaven, instead of water
Through all the air the burning brimstone whirled,
The elements of Hell from Heaven were hurled—
From the pure Heaven—God's holy habitation—
Where angels bow with humble adoration—
Ev'n there the fierceness of His anger swells,
And hate pervades the home in which He dwells;
For fire and brimstone there are made, or stored,
To be in vengeance on His creatures poured:
Men, women, children, doomed by heavenly fire,
Amid these burning cities to expire,
Where smoking embers mingled with the dead,
And all were burned except a few who fled.
Lot's wife amazed, while in her rapid flight
Looked back in pity on the awful sight,
Which of itself would seem to be no fault,
Yet was condemned, and turned at once to salt.)[1]

When golden morn dissolved the silv'ry stars,
And dimmed the polished face of genial Mars,
Before the Sun had kissed the smoky air

---

[1] Gen. xix. 24–26.

That draped in mourning ruins once so fair,
Then Abraham arose, the Lord he found,
Before Him stood, and viewed the smoking
  ground,
Where fire and brimstone mingled with their
  breath,
Amid the last expiring groans of death;
While good old Lot with his two daughters
  fair—[1]
The last fond trio worthy of God's care—
His hopeful seed from which He fain would
  raise
A mighty people to proclaim His praise,
Were so affrighted by the fiery wave,
That buried cities in a molten grave,
They sought a mountain cave in land of Zoar,
That fire and brimstone might disturb no
  more.
There lived this chosen—only righteous three
In undisturbed repose and harmony.

[1] Gen. xix. 27, 28.—[2] xix. 30

Though Lot's fond wife at first was not rejected,
Yet for one look of pity, unsuspected,
Was turned from flesh and blood to rigid salt,
And stood like polished marble by a vault!
But shame and sorrow must pervade each breast,
For daughters thus who were by angels blest,
Who could commit so base, so dark a crime,
And cast their shadows on the sands of time.
My *modest pen and ink are both agreed*,
That if the details you should choose to read,
Please take the record which is not denied,
Peruse and ponder until satisfied.[1]
But sadly strange that every pious soul,
That God designed for His supreme control,
Should yet defy His power and holy will—
That Satan thus should hold dominion still!
But all the sins that darken every fall,
This last surpasses, and disgraces all!

[1] Gen. xix. 31–38.

These vain attempts to rescue man from hell,
And fit him in a better place to dwell,
To stay the surging waves of death and sin,
To bar the gate, and keep the Devil in,
Induced the Lord to compromise and yield,
To cease the contest, and give up the field;
To give His children to the fiend of Hell,
And earth for his abode, with them to dwell;
Securing only one, one only blest,
And make no further effort for the rest;
But give to this supreme and constant care;
This one alone, should all His blessings share,
His seed receive protection everywhere;[1]
While Satan, with his many thousand strong,
With victors' palms, cheered with triumphant song,
Retained the conquest of his captured throng.

Thus Abraham was now God's only seed,
To bear the ensign and maintain His creed,
Yet should his blood all unborn nations know,

[1] Gen. xxii. 15–18.

And God would on them holy love bestow;
Not all the sands on shores of every sea,
Whose numbers almost reach infinity,
Or countless stars that swim in endless space,
Can swell the numbers of this chosen race:
Thus with high hopes the future now was
    planned,
With poor old Abraham at His command!
While Satan, ready with his mighty throng,
To wage another war, when foes were strong;
Yea, eager for the combat soon or late,
When foes for battle fierce might generate.

While thus out-numbered and each effort lost,
Upon the waves of doubt God's hopes were
    tossed,
Despondent shadows veiled the vacant earth
When lo! two nations born at single birth:[1]
To raise a people, God with zeal begins,

---

[1] Gen. xxv. 23.

For who before, or since, hath matched these
    twins!
      Thus barren Rebekah
        Within their pavilions,
      Should be the fond mother
        Of thousands of millions.[1]

Man's days now brief, cut short his stay,
While generations past away
From Abraham to Isaac's race,
Next Jacob followed in his place,
Both were the chosen ones of God,
To represent His will abroad.

But Satan yet busy, beheld with delight,
That foes were increasing made ready for fight.
Like a fiend in disguise, or the tiger that creeps
On innocent prey, while it quietly sleeps,
So Satan in ambush thus warily came
To Jacob's own mother, Rebekah by name;
And taught this fond parent the truth to deny—

[1] Gen. xxiv. 60.

To cheat poor old Isaac—taught Jacob to lie!
To rob her son Esau of blessings in store;
The child of her bosom, she honestly bore.[1]
Poor Esau dejected, in sorrow then cried,
"O father, do bless me, why am I denied?
Shall Jacob thus rob me by artful deceit,
By willfully lying, thy blessing defeat?
Remember, dear father, my birthright he craved,
Now robs me of all you so graciously saved."

But too late was his plea, all tears were in vain;[2]
No prayers could avail, what was done must remain.

While Esau defeated and robbed of his right,
We'll not forget Jacob, but see in what light
We view him while proud of his ill-gotten weal;

[1] Gen. xxvii. 33.—[2] xxvii. 34–36.

But readily see the dark shadows that steal
O'er the wreck of his hopes, defying repose,
While justice condemns him wherever he goes:
Oh, view him while taught by his mother to lie,
To rob his own brother, his visage deny;
With heart so corrupted and conscience thus
    seared,
Deceiving his father he should have revered.
Who can envy his lot? No contentment is
    there,
His pleasures like bubbles will burst in the air.
With ill-gotten treasures, no blessings can bless,
No tongue can console, and no hand can caress.

But poor honest Esau is richer tenfold,
Than Jacob with caskets of coral and gold;
With conscience approving and loving the right,
Wherever he journeyed it gave him delight.

But lo, as we trace the dark shadows that
    roll,

Enshrouding the senses, misleading the soul;
So clouding the light from the fountain on high,
That God is beheld with a half-seeing eye.
And then so distorted and misunderstood,
He sanctions the evil as though it were good.
Behold Him as seen blessing Jacob who lied,[1]
Who robbed his own brother and father beside;
See the plot of deception to ruin his brother,
Concocted and taught by his own wicked mother.[2]
No censure for mother or son can we trace;
Unfortunate record, misleading the race;
But God, as reported, confirms the foul deed,
By blessing this Jacob and all of his seed![3]

But Jacob with riches and honor prevailed,
While treasures of Laban he wrongly assailed,
And with them departed too much like a thief,
But God yet sustained him, which gave him relief,

[1] Gen. xxviii 14, 15.—[2] xxvii.—[3] xxviii. 14, 15.

And still would be with him whate'er might
    befall,
With ring-streaked cattle and asses and all.[1]

Thus Jacob prevailing in every design,
The line of his power he could not define.
With courage unbounded and will undenied,
All mortals outrivaled, while God he defied.
Preposterous thought, yet as *true as the book*,
A wrestle with God he next undertook![2]
At night's gentle stillness, while nature reposed,
And all but the stellar worlds quietly dozed,
This Jacob and God, each contending for
    power,
Selected the silent and slumbering hour,
To prove to the world as the end might befall,
Which one should be monarch and master of all.

The contest seemed doubtful while night swiftly
    sped,

[1] Gen. xxx. 27–43; xxxi. 1–3.—[2] xxxii. 24–30.

'Till twilight of morning o'er Nature was shed;
While Jacob, less yielding than darkness of
   night,
Was hopeful, determined, in excellent plight;
When God without hope to successfully vie
Used Jacob unfairly, disjointing his thigh:
But Jacob unyielding, though crippled and
   lame,
Yet hopeful for conquest, still wrestled the
   same,
And held Him so closely, so firm in his power,
That God from this moment, beginning to cower,
Exclaimed, "Let me go, the daylight is break-
   ing.'
For thou hast prevailed in this undertaking."
Victorious Jacob denied God's petition,
But still would release Him on certain condition;
The terms God accepted, and Jacob succeeded
In winning the game and all blessings he
   needed.[2]

[1] Gen. xxxii. 25, 26.—[2] xxxii. 29.

Behold the great Author of all that we scan,
Is thwarted by Satan, out-wrestled by man.
God said, "As a prince I acknowledge thy power,
Thy name shall be honored from this very hour,
As with man so with Me thy success is the same,
I'll call thee not Jacob but Israel's thy name."[1]
Thus ended the contest without reservation,
While Jacob was monarch of all God's creation!

The rolling years in their resistless flight,
Like twilight shadows on the verge of night,
Sped swiftly on, not heeding weal or woe,
As floating clouds before the tempest go;
And while the ancient record we pursue,
A God distorted still is brought to view;
And His most hopeful seed, arrayed in power
Again are thwarted in an evil hour:

[1] Gen. xxxii. 28.

Thus Jacob,. once so richly clad and fed,
Came near starvation's brink for want of bread;
And all his tribes, Jehovah's chosen race,
Are headlong hurled from their exalted place,
And doomed to serve the *servants of the devil*,
A God-forsaken race, whose hope was evil;
And were oppressed by them in servile chains,
While Pharaoh, king of Egypt, held the reins.
Thus slavery with its heinous crimes was born,
To make despairing hope still more forlorn:
It seems that God ordained the institution,
Made Pharaoh's will the law and constitution;
And fearing he might let his slaves depart,
God often hardened Pharaoh's wicked heart;
Thus passed long years, while hope was yet deferred,
Of chains that bound them, not a link was stirred,
No voice for freedom rent the burdened air,
No ray of light in this their dark despair.

But lo! a mother who her babe must hide,[1]
In ark of rushes launched him on the tide,
Amid the dangers there alone to ride:
No gentle voice to soothe, nor hand to save,
His little bark was rocked by every wave;
The evening zephyrs sang his lullaby,
Though every breeze that murmured was a sigh.
Yet from that feeble floating cradle-bed,
Sprang Israel's hope, and only promised head,
Yea, Moses rose by Infinite decree,
Their chains to break and set the nation free;[2]
He came commissioned by the will of God,
To rule King Pharaoh with a magic rod;
A strange collision here we plainly see,
While God through Pharaoh said it should
    not be;[3]
God sent the plagues to melt his stubborn heart,
To make him yield, that Israel might depart,
While oft subdued and filled with grief and
    pain,

[1] Ex. ii. 2,3.—[2] iii. 15-18.—[3] iv. 21.

The monarch's heart was hardened yet again;
Like as the smith who works with cheerful zeal,
First heats his rod to make the hardened steel

Now Moses was a meek and honest man,
And sought no part in this two-sided plan;
For as God chose to harden Pharaoh's heart,
On his new mission he was loath to start;[1]
The Lord to give him courage in command,
Instructed him in tricks at sleight of hand,
And turned his rod into a running snake;
Alarmed, he fled with haste for safety's sake;[2]
Then God to Moses said, with much avail,
Put forth thy hand and take it by the tail;
The tail he caught, nor was it caught in vain,
The frightful snake became a rod again.[3]

But Moses yet reluctantly declined,
For fear his tongue would not express his
    mind;[4]

[1] Ex iv. 1.—[2] iv. 2,3.—[3] iv. 4.—[4] iv. 10.

God much enraged, thus failing to persuade
    him,
Sent Aaron with him, as a tongue to aid him;[1]
Thus well equipped with other wondrous things,
He was prepared to meet the face of kings.
Still God, distrusting Moses, sought his life,
And met him by the way in deadly strife;[2]
But as the Lord in bloody combat failed,
He chose to have the king by him assailed;
And forth to Pharaoh went with magic rod,
To prove by tricks that he was sent from
    God;[3]
That He who made the heavens, the earth,
    and sea,
Hath said that Israel's children must be free.

Soon, face to face, did they with Pharaoh meet,
And Aaron cast the rod before his feet:
Presto change! in serpent form it crawled;
But Pharaoh quickly *his* magicians called,

[1] Ex. iv. 14-16.—[2] iv. 24.—[3] vii. 10.

Who came with rods and threw them on the
    ground,
When *each* became a serpent running round.
Thus in this *first* act Moses was defeated,
For all that he had done was well repeated[1]

But Moses next with rod assailed the flood,
The fishes died, and waters turned to blood;
Yet the magicians led by Pharaoh's will,
Performed the same with their unfailing skill:[2]
Which seemed to prove that Moses, with his
    rod,
Might not have seen, or ever heard of God.

But Aaron next with rod in outstretched
    hand,
Invited all the frogs upon the land;
Yet the magicians with like magic skill,
Called up the frogs obedient to their will:[3]
Till all the realm was filled in every place,

Ex. vii. 10–12.—[2] vii. 19–22.—[3] viii. 5–7.

With this amphibious, hopping, croaking race.
Now Pharaoh being over-run with frogs,
Implored they might return among the bogs,
If God complied all Israel then might go—
Be ever free from daily toil and woe.
But now his hardened heart by God's decree,
Forbade that Israel's children should be free:
For when he saw the croakers disappear,
He broke his vow, and did not God revere.[1]

Next Aaron with his rod assailed the dust,
And all the grains upon the earth's fair crust
Were turned to lice, by God's *divine* command,
To show His mighty power throughout the land:[2]
Egyptian skill which heretofore prevailed,
In this *great lousy trick completely failed;*[3]

[1] Ex viii. 8-15—[2] viii. 17.—[3] viii. 18.

And the magicians did at length determine
That none but Moses' God could make the vermin![1]
Yet Pharaoh's hardened heart, by God's decree
Forbade that Israel's children should be free.

INTERLUDE.

(Though hard or soft his heart, who could consent
To yield the palm, and sorrowing relent,
And love this God, and venerate His name,
While thrice defeated in a chosen game?
And though surpassed by God in making lice,
He need not envy Him in that device,
Yet we admit (make much of the admission),
That God (so called) was but the best magician!)

While Moses now Egyptian skill outvies,
He fills the land with grievous swarms of flies.[2]
Next all the cattle by divine command,

[1] Ex. viii. 19.—[2] viii. 24.

He smote with murrain throughout all the land,[1]
While boils and blains afflicted Pharaoh's race,[2]
And groans and sighs were heard in every place.
Then followed hail with intermingled fire,
Which smote with death, fulfilling God's desire:
Till Pharaoh cried, "It is enough! forbear!
These all combined are more than mortal's share.
If fire and hail and roaring thunders cease,
All Israel's children I will then release."[3]

INTERLUDE.

(Pray pity him who fain would let them go,
But God ordained that it should not be so;
Then blame him not while bound by firm decree,

[1] Ex. ix. 3-7.—[2] , ix. 8-10.—[3] , ix. 22-28.

That Israel's children yet should not be free!
For He who raised him up, and gave him birth
To show His mighty power throughout the earth,
Would not consent that Pharaoh's heart should yield,
Until His horrid purpose was revealed;
That Pharaoh still must suffer grief and pain,
For only doing what God did ordain.[1]
That "God of love" might show what He hath willed,
Then damn His child through whom it was fulfilled.
What other course, I ask, could he pursue,
When all he did, God raised him up to do?
And can you say, (Oh, say it not to me)!
That this is God who fills immensity?
If this be so, wherever I may dwell,
Unending space to me is endless hell!)

Next swarming clouds of locusts filled the land,[2]

[1] Ex. ix. 16; x. 1,2.—[2] x. 12-16.

To eat the scattered grain the hail let stand,
And to devour all vegetation fair,
And leave earth's bosom desolate and bare.

Next darkness came, and like a funeral pall,
With mantle thick and black, enveloped all;
And hung o'er vegetation's corpse a gloom,
A darkness ten times darker than the tomb,
For three long days without a ray of light:
Where was the sun in this protracted night?[1]
But Pharaoh, now again, as oft before,
Called unto Moses, whom he did implore;
And said, "Now go from Egypt with your sons,
Your wives and daughters, and your little ones;
And only let your flocks and herds be stayed:
In leaving them you will not be delayed."[2]

Without his herds he would not leave the sod
For they must burn a sacrifice to God.
A cattle's hoof shall not remain behind,

[1] Ex. x. 20–23—[2] x. 24.

Without reserve these were the terms defined.[1]

And while the king made ready to reply,
To yield the point, or else perhaps deny,
God seemed to fear his hardened heart would fail,
That Moses and the plagues might now prevail;
And fearing Israel's children might depart,
Again re-hardened Pharaoh's hardened heart;[2]
Thus vetoed all, and took direct command,
To multiply His wonders in the land.
God said to Moses, "Pharaoh shall not hear[3]
(And hearing not, he surely could not fear),
That I may bring upon him one plague more,[4]
Eclipsing all I ever did before.
He then will give you all a glad release,
And let your flocks and herds depart in peace;
But now, before you make this move so bold,

[1] Ex x. 25, 26.—[2] x. 27.—[3] xi. 9.—[4] xi. 1, 9.

First borrow all their silver and their gold,
I'll give thee favor in their doubtful eyes,[1]
That they may not the borrower despise.
And I, the Lord, before the early dawn,
Will smite in Egypt all of her first born."[2]

O mortals, lend your ears! What rends the air?[]
What cries and groans so full of deep despair?
Is half a nation wailing for the dead?
Have all their cherished hopes forever fled?
Is every home made desolate and bare?
And every mother frantic with despair?
An awful chorus freights the midnight air![4]

But read the page, its import ponder well,
If this be God, where is the fiend of Hell?
For God (so called) and maker of the race,
Came forth at midnight from His holy place,[5]
While mothers slept, with infants on their
    breast,

[1] Ex. xi. 2, 3.—[2] xi. 4, 5.—[3] xi. 6.—[4] xii. 30.—[5] xii. 29

In calm repose upon their couch of rest—
My pen now falters while I trace the lines,
Where God is falsely charged with base designs:
But reason's light should guide the man who reads—
That God of love with bloody hands proceeds
To every house, before the early dawn,
To slay in Egypt all of her first born;
That throughout Israel, whether old or young,
No harm shall come, no dog shall move his tongue;
Their very beasts He will protect with care,
While babes of Egypt shall His vengeance share;
That ye may know that He who all controls,
Thinks more of Israel's dogs, than Egypt's souls![1]

To guard His chosen few, with care selected,

[1] Ex. xi. 7.

Their homes were stained with blood and thus
    protected,
That God might pass them by without mistake,
While murd'ring infants for His GLORY'S
    SAKE![1]
First born of kings obedient to His will,
First born of maids that served behind the
    mill,
First born of captives in the dungeon bound,
First born of all, where blood could not be
    found,
Alike He slew, as first of every beast,[2]
God's flaming vengeance surely had a feast!

INTERLUDE.

(If every demon, filled with awful rage,
Should burst the confines of his smoky cage,
And rush with heated fury from his cell,
And leave behind a quiet, vacant hell;
Should pile the horrors of that dismal clime,

[1] Ex. xii. 22, 23.—[2] xi. 5; xii. 29.

With all its terrors at a given time
Upon a race, while couched in quiet sleep,
While midnight slumbers locked their senses deep;
They could but shadow forth (don't call it true),
What God performed, what demons could not do!
Is this the God whose mercies from above
Exhibit tender and paternal love,
Who left His throne on high and came to earth,
And took the form of man, in humble birth?
Who left the glories of a heaven most high,
To bear His cross, to suffer shame and die,
To rescue man from an eternal hell,
And fit his soul for heaven, where angels dwell!
Is this the Lord who lovingly caressed
The little children, whom He took and blest?
If so, a glorious change for man is wrought:
But can a changing God, with hope be sought?)

But we'll return to Pharaoh, though with pain,
And briefly trace him through his fearful reign.
While viewing murdered babes on every side,
Whose throbbing hearts revealed a crimson tide,
While mothers' groans, re-echoed from the ground

In frantic discords, rent the air around,
Though God again had made his heart like
    steel,
In spite of all, he now was made to feel;
Yea, more, to act: without an hour's delay,
He ordered Israel's children sent away;
And called to Moses while it yet was night,
And said, "I pray thee, make a speedy flight,
With all of Israel, leaving not a head,
And freely serve the Lord as ye have said;[1]
All must depart, or we are surely dead:
Your cattle and your herds, leave none behind,
These are the terms that you yourself defined."
And to secure a prompt and speedy start,
They freely did with gold and raiment part;
Thus one and all from Pharaoh were set free,
Away they wound their journey to the sea.

All Egypt now reposed in quiet rest,
Without a plague to hinder or molest;

[1] Ex. xii. 29-33.

Hope sweetly smiled, yet all their hopes were vain,
For God now hardened Pharaoh's heart again,
And sent him forth to capture and subdue,
And to this end with vigor did pursue.
With ten times hardened heart by God's decree,
He followed Israel's children to the sea;
And found them all encamped upon the shore,
Where rolling tides obstructed them before.[1]
But He who led them forth by clouds of fire,
Through Egypt's wilds, 'mid dangers dark and dire,
Had now aroused all Egypt from their rest,
And put a fiery demon in each breast.
With crowded chariots drawn by foaming steeds,
They dashed with fury on for valiant deeds,
To capture Israel, as they all supposed;
But just before they in fierce combat closed,

[1] Ex. xiv. 4–9.

God interfered ere yet they reached the scene,
By clouds of darkness sent to intervene.[1]
Thus were they hampered by the very hand
That raised their hopes, while death was only
    planned;
For while God hemmed their pathway by a
    cloud,
He was preparing for them each a shroud—
Was opening wide and deep a watery grave
Below the angry surface of the wave—
While o'er the pathway leading through the
    sea,
Marched Israel in safety, and was free.[2]
The darkened clouds now lift their curtain-
    folds,
And Pharaoh with astonished gaze beholds,
Amid the deep, a path from shore to shore,
Where Israel walks in safety on before.
While Pharaoh now beheld the vacant main,
His hardened heart, God hardened yet again;[3]

[1] Ex. xiv. 20.—[2] xiv. 21, 22.—[3] xiv. 17.

With sinews steeled he now pursued his foes,
Not dreaming that the Lord would interpose,
But God who had inspired his hope with zeal
Was now prepared His motive to reveal—
To prove to him, while in the watery gap,
That Moses was the *bait* and *this* the *trap!*
Thus God descends from His supernal arch,
To intercept him in his ordered march;
Takes off his chariot wheels while moving round,[1]
And throws the loaded axles on the ground:
Thus while obedient in his wild pursuit,
His steeds were still, and every wheel was mute.
While in this awful plight amid the sea,
With one accord they would from Israel flee.
But God who made their graves so long and deep,
Though sad their fate, resolved His vow to keep,

---

[1] Ex. xiv. 25.

Now broke the bands that held the fearful
    wall:
Then rushed the maddened waters in their fall;
Wave leaped on wave, then broke upon the
    shore,
While every breeze a wail of terror bore;
The angry waters sealed their silent doom,
And gulfed them all within this fearful tomb.

INTERLUDE.

(Thus perished Pharaoh in the deep Red Sea:
There let him rest with long tranquillity;
Remote from plagues—the instruments of God;
Remote from Moses with his magic rod;
Remote from lice, that countless, tireless race;
Remote from frogs, that croaked in every place;
Remote from hissing snakes, that bite and crawl;
Remote from flies, that tease and vex us all;
Remote from maddened hail with fire and smoke;
Remote from boils and blains, that most provoke·
Remote from murdered babes on every side,

[1] Ex. xiv. 26.

Whose weeping mothers would have gladly died;
Remote from God (I hope), who raised him up,
To put these plagues within his bitter cup,
That He might show great wisdom in the deed,
And thus be honored by His chosen seed.

Honor? O shame! The word is stained with crime,
And wrested from a pinnacle sublime.
And God, the name I ever have adored,
Is clothed with all the terrors Hell hath stored!
For He surpasses Satan and his host,
In deeds of which they all combined would boast;
Thus Satan, in this wonder-working age,
Contents himself within his smoky cage,
For God, who first defied his powerful arm,
So oft subdued, now seems to yield the palm;
And rather than again oppose his will,
Does *Satan's work to keep old Satan still!*

Pray do not censure him who writes these lines,
It is not he who thus the Lord defines:
But read the page with an unbiased mind,
And more than here is penned, you there will find:
All there may see that God in very deed,
In Pharaoh's movements always took the lead,
Ordained his course and nerved his hardened heart,

That he could not from His decrees depart;[1]
That for this purpose God had raised him up,
And deeply filled his burning, bitter cup;
That He in him might plainly show to man,
An undisputed record of His plan;
And thus acquire a wondrous reputation
Throughout the world, in every tribe and nation.
As rivers run within their channels deep,
'Mid flowery meads, or cataracts to leap,
So Pharaoh, led by Him who shaped his mind,
Could not forsake the path that was defined;
But gladly wound his way through weal and woe—
Through storm and sunshine, facing every foe;
Yet strange to say, while serving God so well,
The path he trod, should end in ENDLESS HELL!)

But Moses and his tribe with one accord,[2]
Proclaimed a glorious triumph of the Lord:
Thus praised his name because their crue
    foes
Beneath the waves had found their last repose
" The Lord is our defense and man of war;
O praise His holy name forever more!

[1] Ex. ix. 16; Rom. ix. 17.—[2] Ex. xv. 1-10.

For He in greatness, goodness, and in wrath,
Consumes all foes, like stubble in His path:
And with the blasts that from His nostrils sweep,
Walls in the floods, and stays the rolling deep.

  For the depths were congealed
  In the heart of the sea,
  And our path was revealed
  To the land of the free!

And as we safely reached the happy shore,
Our foes pursued, but God, with one breath more,
Released the flood, the restless foaming tide,
Where Pharaoh and his hosts together died.
O praise the Lord in one grand chorus swell,
For saving us, and sending them to hell."
Thus Moses sang on old Arabia's shore,
While murdering waves their chimes of terror bore.

INTERLUDE.

(All Israel now released from hostile foes,
Exempt from Egypt's bondage and its woes,
Breathed freedom's holy air, surcharged with hope,
Amid Arabia's wilds with ample scope.
This wand'ring race—the chosen tribe of God,
Still led by Moses, with his magic rod,
Freed from the terrors of internal foes,
With none but Satan left to interpose,
Why may they not become a race more pure,
If God hath power the devil to secure;
Or can to some extent His plans fulfill,
If not to conquer Satan, keep him still?
We fain would hope at this eventful day,
That Israel's God might have triumphant sway.
But read the page, be honest while you seek,
Nerved for the right, let truth and reason speak!)

As Israel journeyed from the sea-girt shore,[1]
A hopeful future cheered them as before:
But, sad to tell, they soon were plunged within

[1] Ex. xv. 22.

A dark abyss—the wilderness of Sin.
Grieved to the heart, with lamentations wild,
They sighed for mother Egypt like a child.
"Oh! would to heaven we had in Egypt died,
By God's own hand, with flesh-pots by our side:[1]
Is this the promised land for Israel's race—
This wilderness of Sin, this dismal place?
Where gormand famine preys on old and young,
And gives no drop to cool the burning tongue.
Oh! give us back our childhood's home again,
With Egypt's plagues, with slavery's galling chain."
Thus Israel murmured and with one accord
They censured Aaron, Moses, and the Lord.
To ease their hunger and appease their wrath,
The showers of bread from heaven pursued their path;
And quails, most rich in flavor, winged their flight

[1] Ex. xvi. 3.

Around their tents before the hours of night.[1]
For forty years they were released from toil,
Not having need to cultivate the soil.
God thus repealed His law, so gravely said,
"With sweat upon thy face, shalt thou eat bread."[2]

INTERLUDE.

(We do not choose in this our brief review,
Their line of march in detail to pursue;
Nor trace all wayward paths these men have trod,
Who charge their crimes upon their maker God:
But glean enough to prove the Lord defined,
Was but the passion of each writer's mind;
That all these tribes in this barbarian age,
Reflect but their true image on each page;
That God of vengeance and of wrath unveils,
Only as love within each spirit fails—
And he who loves the Lord of Israel's race,
In this enlightened age is out of place:
He should have lived and died in ages past,

---

[1] Ex. xvi. 12, 13.—[2] Gen. iii. 19.

Ere reason's light its golden hues had cast
Where mortals sat in darkness, free from doubt,
All dimly dreaming what they were about;
When light of science had no resting-place
Within this half-developed human race.
O Reason! in thy searchings look them out,
Arouse their souls and make them dare to doubt;
Teach them to love, and only seek the truth,
Though it may change all lessons taught in youth;
Throw off their shackles, set the trammeled free,
And make them dare to think, and learn of thee!)

While Israel (led by Moses) journeyed on,
Before three months of forty years were gone,[1]
They all approached Mount Sinai's fearful base,
Where God proposed to show his shining face.
While camped near Sinai, Moses upward trod,
And scaled the mountain height and *called on God*:[2]
Who well received him and rehearsed His deeds,
Spake of the present and of future needs:
And said that Israel should behold His face,[3]

[1] Ex. xix. 1.—[2] xix. 3.—[3] xix. 11-16.

'Mid fire and smoke His features they should
    trace.
But all must wash and make their garments
    clean,
Before the Lord on Sinai could be seen:
Three days were granted by the Lord's decree,
That they might one and all from filth be free.
When the third morning winged its silent
    round,
Old Sinai's roaring thunders shook the ground,
And forked lightning's lurid, leaping flame,
Cut loose its reins and sped from whence it
    came,
All Isreal now beheld with wond'ring eyes,
The fire and smoke, while thunders shook the
    skies;
They stood amazed, yet sought in vain God's face,
For neither form or feature could they trace.

Hope thus deferred, well might their doubts arise[1]

[1] Ex. xviii.

And on reflection thus soliloquize;
"If this *is* Moses' God with such a face,
He is not *ours*, in this, or any place;
If 'tis not God, then Moses did deceive,
Or God hath said what we can not believe;
Be as it may, the case to us is clear,
A God like that we never can revere;
We would prefer a molten god by half,
Though molded in the image of a calf."[1]

But strange to say that seventy-four in all,[2]
Went bravely up, and gave the Lord a call.
They saw His feet, on pavement made of stone;
While all His form with heavenly clearness
    shone.
God said to Moses, "Say to Israel's tribe,
'Tis my desire that they for me subscribe:
I'll take of them what they may give to thee;
Gold, silver, brass, or any thing it be,
Blue cloth or purple, goat's hair, too, is good,

[1] Ex. xxxii. 1-4.— [2] xxiv. 9-11.

Rams' skins in red, spices, and shittim wood."
Much more He wished, and hoped that they would give,
Beside a house, where He might come and live,
To make His home and constant dwelling-place,
Among these wayward tribes of Israel's race.¹

INTERLUDE.

O world of mortals, men of high repute,
Is this your God? speak—are you deaf and mute?
If silence doth affirm, and yield consent,
And from your thoughtless souls it giveth vent,
Pray let me ask you to reflect a while,
And see how Nature's God you all defile.
Is this the Author of the beauteous earth?
Who gave all other worlds their form and birth?
Who made our stellar orbs that, one by one,
Revolve in order round their parent sun?
Made worlds on worlds revolve around each star,
In silent grandeur, all without a jar?
Who marshalled all the glitt'ring orbs of light,
Gave each its path, and never-ending flight?

¹ Ex xxv. 1-9; xxix.

Who gave to Saturn his concentric rings,
Within whose golden bands he whirls and swings!
Thus suns and systems tread the depths of space,
And leave no tracks for other worlds to trace.
Unending spheres revolve 'mid viewless skies,
 Till lost in thought, imagination dies;
Yet all united, all one law obey,
Like little wheels that keep the time of day;
All speak one language to th' enraptured ear,
To every clime, that nature's God is here:
That He who governs all with constant care,
Records his glorious image everywhere.

O God of nature, infinite in power,
Thy wisdom shines more radiant every hour;
Yet none but Thou canst ever comprehend
Thy wondrous works, though ages never end.
Thy boundless being circles all extent,
Thy will, all worlds and beings represent;
The viewless shores of Thine eternal sea,
Are gemmed with worlds that know no God but
 Thee.
Yet thoughtless, weak, irreverential man,
Hath such delusive vision of Thy span,
That he would measure Thee with square and rule,
As he now takes dimensions of a mule;

Hath such uncouth conceptions of Thy head,
He makes Thee covet ram skins dyed in red;
Would wall Thy boundless limits to a house.
As children capture and incage a mouse!)

But Moses tarried long on Sinai's mount;[1]
For which delay they could not well account;
And fearing he might not return again,
And as desires to see the Lord proved vain,
The people said, "Up, Aaron! make a god
To lead us on, like Moses with his rod."
So Aaron—like the priests of modern times,
Who preach for gold, or even for the dimes,
And to this end preach what the people will,
Or any god, so they but get their fill—
Obeyed their voice, their most preposterous plea,
And made a god, that they could feel and see,
Of golden rings, from out their jeweled ears,
A molten god, of which they had no fears.[2]
When Aaron smoothed it off with graven tool,
He told them with an air of truth so cool,

[1] Ex. xxxii. 1.—[2]. xxxii. 2, 3.

"This is the god that took direct command,
That led you forth from Egypt's darkened
    land;"
Then built an altar, made a proclamation,
Declared the calf the god of all that nation.[1]

When Moses' God the golden calf beheld,
And saw the people joyfully impelled
To bow before this legged lump of gold,
And that by such a calf His throne was sold.
He said to Moses, "Get thee down, I pray,
The people have departed from their way;[2]
Let me alone to act my chosen part,
And sate the vengeance of my burning heart,
For all my wrath against them waxed hot,
And I'll consume them all upon the spot;
But out of thee I'll make a nation great—
Restore the race to its primeval state."[3]

But Moses, not elated by this plea,

[1] Ex. xxxii. 4, 5.—[2] xxxii. 7, 8.—[3] xxxii. 10, 11.

Would not consent to let Jehovah be;
But chose to pacify His wrathful zeal,
And thus addressed Him till he made Him feel:
"If thus Thine anger burns and waxes hot,
And sure destruction is their doleful lot,
All Egypt then will speak, and justly say,
That God *designed* His people here to slay.
Turn from Thy fearful wrath, at once repent
Before Thy vengeance is on Israel spent;
Remember Abraham, and Isaac too;
And what Thou swearest by Thyself to do—
To multiply their seed like stars of heaven;
A promised land should unto them be given;
And all their seed inherit it forever,
From which no power their title deed should sever."[1]

Thus Moses intercepts Him in the path,
Controls His will, and stays that awful wrath.

[1] Ex. xxxii. 11-13.

And God repents of evil thought to do,
And spares the golden calf and Israel too.[1]

The Lord diverted from such fearful ways,
The threatened vengeance for a while delays;
Then Moses turning from Him left the mount,
Came down to Israel from the fiery fount,
With stones, containing God's divine command.
All written o'er, within his grasping hand:
Approaching Israel, songs salute his ear;
The merry dance was seen as he drew near;
The golden calf appeared amid the throng,
And all the air re-echoed with their song.

Now Moses, though he preached to God so well,
To save this people and His wrath expel,
Forgot the lesson of an hour before,
And all its moral import did ignore;
His anger, like a rising, rushing tide,
Or red-hot lava from a mountain side,

[1] Ex. xxxii. 14.

Leaped from the slumbers of its quiet rest,
And roused a deadly demon in his breast!
While in this awful plight with God's great .aw,
Celestially engraved without a flaw,
Select as every letter thus must be,
As specimen of God's chirography,
He dashed the graven record from his hands,
And broke in fragments the divine commands,
Then *grabbed* the calf, impelled by heated ire
And cast the golden image in the fire.[2]

The Lord perceiving Moses in such plight,
Employs his wrath to instigate a fight;
To arm each son and speed him on the way
With sword in hand a demon to portray;
Each to his brother, his companion, friend,
A crimson tide from every heart to send.[3]

Now Moses, in his *wrathful* mood, obeyed;
Did not oppose, nor was God's will delayed,

[1] Ex. xxxii. 15–19.—[2] xxxii. 20.—[3] xxxii. 27.

But quickly armed his men for deadly fight,
And waged a bloody combat with delight.
There fell three thousand, as the record stands,[1]
Of friends and kindred by the Lord's commands:
Thus broke Himself His law, "Thou shalt not kill,"
On stones engraved, the record of His will.[2]
If He repented in the *other* place,
He surely must have " fallen now from grace."
And soon from polished etiquette departs—
Conceals His face, but shows *His hindmost parts!* [3]

This ancient God, the pattern of that age,
So oft misled by fierce vindictive rage,
Records His law in chapters long and dry,
Which all can read, we therefore pass them by:
But after full directions what to eat,
And which must be refused in kinds of meat,
How strange the record seems while there we read,

[1] Ex. xxxii 28.—[2] xx. 13.—[3] xxxiii. 23.

That God Himself commands the heinous deed
To eat the flesh of their *own children dear*,
If they did not His horrid laws revere![1]

This God, who also said, "Thou shalt not kill,"
Directed Moses to revoke His will,
And raise a mighty army fierce and bold,
Six hundred thousand strong in numbers told;
To plunge the naked sword and javelin
Against a race of men they had not seen.
This mighty army numb'ring every soul
From age of twenty on their muster roll,[2]
Now left the Mount and took unmeasured route,
Through trackless wilds with mingled hope and doubt.
And as the tide of time then ebbed and flowed,
Upon whose restless waves they swiftly rode,
They often murmured at the hand of fate,
That led them safely through the Red Sea gate.

[1] Lev. xxvi. 29.—[2] Num. i. 1.—46.

VOICE OF SUPERSTITION.

In vain they wished, in spite of quails and bread,
Which heaven in rich abundance freely shed,
That they had all remained in Egypt's land,
Where hardened Pharaoh ruled with iron hand.
But still they journeyed on from year to year,
And yet their promised land did not appear.
Then God directed Moses in this wise—
"Go seek the promised land by sending spies."
Thus twelve departed, one from every band,
To search for "Canaan's fair and happy land!"
For forty days they sought but all in vain;
When each returned to Israel's tribe again.
A part described a land of milk and honey;
With cities large that cost a "mint of money."
But all the rest declared that "giants large,
Ate human flesh—the subjects of their charge;
If we should fall within their ruling power,
Our armies would be swallowed in an hour."[1]

With these reports conflicting in their ears,

[1] Num. xiii.

Amid their hopes, arose perplexing fears;
And all the night the congregation cried—
"Oh, would that we had all in Egypt died!
We'll make another captain and return."
Thus did their murmuring hearts for Egypt burn.[1]

God now in wrath rebukes these homesick
    souls,
And like an avalanche His anger rolls;
And threatens with a pestilential stroke,
To disinherit all who thus provoke.[2]

Again the meek high priest, as oft before,
Approached the Lord, and thus he did im-
    plore:
"If Thou do thus, all Egypt then will hear,
And speak of it in everybody's ear;
For they have heard of Thee throughout the
    place,
And of my talking with Thee face to face;

[1] Num. xiv. 1–4.—[2] xiv. 11, 12.

And of the cloud that led them forth by day,
And fire by night to light their darkened way.
Now if Thou slay them all, where is Thy fame
Among the people who have heard Thy name?
They then will say, what God had sworn to do,
He failed for want of power and wisdom too;
And as He could not lead them in His way,
To stop defeat, He did all Israel slay."[1]

This flattering speech was all that then was needed,
For to it all God willingly acceded.[2]

So Israel journeyed on to Edom's land,
And fought their way with bloody sword in hand:
But much disheartened for the want of meat,
And having naught but loathsome bread to eat,
It was not strange that they should now complain,

---

[1] Num. xiv. 13-17 —[2] xiv. 20.

When God could send them bread and quails
   like rain,
And thus relieve them in their starving plight,
They having served the Lord in every fight:
While hunger gnawed 'twas human to com
   plain,
Yet all their bitter cries and tears were vain,
For God, instead of granting their desire,
Sent poison serpents, made of flaming fire.

While thus tormented, and with sinking heart,
They prayed the heinous reptiles might depart;
But no—God let the vampires live and bite;
They did His work, which gave Him great
   delight:[1]
For though they brought but death and dark
   despair,
'Twas sweet revenge to force the *bill of fare:*
And did not practice what He since hath said,
"If foes are hungered, let them all be fed."[2]

[1] Num. xxi. 6.—[2] Rom. xii. 20.

Amid their torment and distressing fear,
All prayers were vain, that snakes might disappear;
Yet God but mocks their agonizing prayer,
And hangs a brazen serpent high in air;
That all that snakes had bitten might, alas!
Yet live, by seeing Satan cut in brass!
But stranger still, the image of the devil,
Is foreordained, to rescue man from evil!
Thus Satan's form before so much despised,
God now respects; this can not be disguised.[1]

But Israel fought their passage day by day,
And paved with human skulls their winding way;
The crimson tide yet stains the "sacred page,"
While God ignites the flames of deathly rage:
Yea, human slaughter, forced by His decree,
Baptizes earth amid a bloody sea.
Read but the page how Midian's hosts were slain,

[1] Num. xxi. 7-10.

And death's dark mantle veiled the gory
    plain.;
Where every male, from hoary age to youth,
Was murdered in the name of God and truth;[1]
And every female who had known a man,
Was doomed to die, by God's remorseless plan,
Though her warm love in one pure channel
    flowed,
And by a holy union was bestowed,[2]
Affection deep availed no more than hate,
For every loving wife but shared the fate
To swell the bloody wave, the lukewarm tide,
While God beheld the scene and did preside.
But this is not the whole, though dark the
    tale;
Oh, would that pen could penetrate the veil,
Disclose the wrongs that broke poor woman's
    heart,
Exposed her shame, with none to take her
    part.

Num. xxxi. 7.—[2] xxxi. 17.

Each virgin was disrobed by bloody sires,
To gratify their lusts and base desires!
For every woman who knew not a man,
Was *doomed to live* by this licentious clan,
And made to suffer shame to such degree,
That death in mercy would have set them free ![1]
Yet God commanded and enforced the deeds,
If He be not misjudged, for thus it reads,
And shared with them the booty and the glory,—
Thus ends this false and inconsistent story.
With more than thirty thousand virgins spared,
God two from every thousand with them shared ![2]
Of all the sheep, almost a countless throng,
His rightful portion was twelve thousand strong.[3]
Large herds of cattle stand in open view,
Of which the Lord accepted thirty-two,[4]

[1] Num. xxxi. 18.—[2] xxxi. 40.—[3] xxxi. 37.—[4] xxxi. 38.

The asses next divided, all was done,
God's share of these was only sixty-one.[1]

Fair Canaan's race next feels celestial wrath,
And sure destruction follows in their path.
All who survive, His vengeance will destroy,
With stinging hornets giving Israel joy.[2]

Next comes God's lesson in unwholesome meat,
Instructing Israel what they should not eat;
" Of beasts that die of poison or disease
If you should eat 'twill kill by slow degrees.
But give or sell for food to passers-by,
To strangers in the gate, though they may die!
For thou so holy to the Lord thy God,
May poison any stranger from abroad."[3][4]

The Lord now seems to love His chosen race,
Calls them a holy people to their face.

[1] Num. xxxi. 39.—[2] Deut. vii. 20.—[3] xiv. 21.
[4] I was a *stranger* and ye *took me in !*—Mat. xxv. 35.

How changed in tone from passage near at hand,
Where God to Moses issues a command,
"To take His chosen leaders every one,
And hang their heads on high against the sun—
Before His face, to hang no other way,
That His fierce anger might not longer stay."[1]
If this command was really obeyed,
And every head against the sun was staid,
Their heads and necks (as they survived the shock)
Must have been made of quite *superior stock*
Be as it may, if God from wrath was cured
By this device, the pain was well endured.
But as we turn our eyes from page to page,
He yet is armed with stern vindictive rage,
Possessing passions of a demon dire,
A jealous God with anger mixed with fire.[2]
With flames decending to the lowest hell,

---

[1] Num. xxv. 4.—[2] Deut. xxxii. 21.

Now dooms His children He had loved so
    well :
Heaps mischief on them all, with arrows sped,
To fly at random from his storming head.
His anger still with wild excitement burns,[1]
On every phase of human life it turns,
Devouring hunger, and the flames of heat,
With bitter death doth all their hopes defeat;
The teeth of beasts shall come upon them all,
And poison serpents round them bite and
    crawl.
The sword of death no age nor station spares,
Young men nor maidens, sucklings, nor gray
    hairs.[2]

But Moses now, with Canaan full in view,
With one fond look, must bid the land adieu.
The dropping sands of time through weary years,
With blighted hopes and mingled doubts and
    fears,

[1] Deut. xxxii 22, 23 —[2] xxxii. 24, 25.

Have chilled the blood that fired his youthful hand,
And changed his footsteps to a better land.
Thus Moses yielded up his mortal life,
And bid adieu to that dark age of strife.[1]

So ended Moses and his sad career;
But now his bold successor doth appear,
To lead the tribes in their appointed way,
The son of Nun, whose name was Joshua.[2]
While thus commissioned with command entire,
He sent two spies full knowledge to acquire.
To Jericho they quickly did repair,
And with a *harlot* took their lodgings there.[3]

As men are judged by company they keep,
The king concluded he would *take a peep*
At these suspicious men, who pleasure sought,
Where empty bubbles are so dearly bought.
But Rahab (being such the harlot's name)

---

[1] Deut. xxxiv. 1, 5.—[2] Josh. i.—[3] ii. 1.

Concluded she would foil him in his game,
And told the king the men had gone their way—
Passed through the gate, when evening closed the day.
She now to make them safe her wits did tax,
And hid them on the roof among the flax.[1]

When twilight shadows veiled the distant plain,
And hung their sable curtains o'er the main,
When all was hushed in quiet peaceful rest,
Except the throbbings of her anxious breast,
She went upon the roof without a fear,
That capped the borders of the city here,
With cord in hand—with muscles firm and true
She let them down, their journey to pursue.
They safely wound their way to Israel's tribes;
Their three days' mountain range no pen describes.

[1] Josh. ii. 2-6.—[2] ii. 15.

To Joshua they did *enough* reveal,
To fire his passions with unholy zeal.
Who, with his tribes faced Jordan's rolling tide,
Its deep intruding waters he defied.
The priests, with ark of covenant before,
Walked through dry shod, and reached the other shore;
The hosts of Israel followed one and all,
While Jordan, like an adamantine wall,
Piled high its limpid waves without a fall!
Thus safely marched the tribes from shore to shore,
Like passing through the space where swings a door.[1]

To make this record true among the nations
In coming years to future generations,
They took twelve stones from out the channel deep,

[1] Josh. iii.

And left them where they tarried first to sleep;
The stones should there remain, as proof for-
    ever,
To mark the spot where Israel crossed the
    river.[1]
This wondrous tale we may believe or not,
For who hath seen the stones, or found the spot!

Ordained of God to wade in human gore,
His vengeance feasted now, as oft before;
Men, women, children, aged, all were slain,[2]
Their supplications rent the air in vain.
But there was one more favored than the rest,
Whom Joshua and all his legions blest;
Her life was guarded well with anxious care,
While carnage hushed the wailings of despair.
And yet this favored one, oh, strange to tell,
Was but a prostitute they loved so well.
God chose these tribes to represent His will,
They chose a harlot, and He loved them still.

[1] Josh. iv. 3-9.—[2] vi. 21.—[3] 21-25.

And yet sustained this base and cruel throng,
Whose deeds are praised in story and in song.[1]
This mighty army under God's command,
Was first on earth that had a music-band,
Composed of priests, with rams' horns seven of each,
Enough all tones in music's scale to reach.
This frightful chorus led the winding way,
And round and round the city walls did play;
For seven long days they blew their awful blast,
While on the seventh, they seven times round it passed;
With thirteen rounds they rent the burdened air,
Like frenzied fiends from regions of despair;
No wonder that the walls of Jericho,
In their imploring attitude laid low.[2]
Though they defied the gnawing tooth of time,

[1] Josh. xxi. 27.—[2] vi. 13-20.

They bowed submissive at this awful chime!
Then leaped these thirsty tribes for human
    blood
Within the walls where this doomed city stood.

INTERLUDE.

(Oh, can it be that men revere the page,
And take their lessons from that barbarous age,
Where God lays bare His arm from shore to shore,
That men may murder those unknown before,
And save the only one they ever knew—
A harlot, for that vile, licentious crew,
Yet represents that God sustains it all,
Though by their hands all but herself may fall!
I may believe that rams' horns shook the ground,
That massive walls from their foundation bound,
Or that the earth itself turned inside out,
When priests with rams' horns mingled in the shout,
But never can I entertain the thought,
A "God of love" these horrid scenes hath wrought.)

But deeds of death still paint the page,
And God of Israel, full of rage,
Yet urges on His heartless band,

To desolate that happy land.
To Ai next the Lord said, Go,
And shroud the land in death and woe,
As dark as hung o'er Jericho.
Thus thirty thousand armed for fight,
By Joshua were sent at night;
And by a bold strategic plan,
They took the life of every man,
Except the king, they saved alive,
But if he had a hope revive,
They soon the rising impulse checked,
And showed him what he might expect;
They hung him high upon a tree,
The first that they perchance did see.[1]

The Gibeonites with one accord,[2]
Now joined with Israel and the Lord,
To save their royal cities strong,
That they their lives might thus prolong.
Five kings then made their armies one,

[1] Josh. viii. 28, 29.—[2] ix.

Declaring war on Gibeon:
In hopes that they with one command,
Might make a strong successful stand.

But Gibeon's united host,
And Father, Son, and Holy Ghost
(If three are one, and one is three,
Then God alone is Trinity),
With Joshua were all combined,
That desolation now might wind
Its fearful path among the kings,
To slay them all like little things.
And for this end, to make it sure,
The Lord from heaven, Himself secure,
Sent down large stones their blood to shed,
And strewed the ground with countless dead.
Then held the golden orb of day,
That round our planet *seems* to play;
Thus barred the sable veil of night,
While He with pleasure held the light,

[1] Josh. x. 1-11.

To strengthen and protract the fight,
To see the fount of human gore,
Its still-increasing flood out pour.[1]
The rolling waves extended wide,
With desolation on the tide,
While o'er the scene He did preside.
Their mournful cries the breezes bore
With sadness to the distant shore.
Thus fell Makkedah in its bloom,
And Libnah, Gezer, shared the doom,
While Eglon, Hebron, Debir, all
Alike were doomed, alike did fall.
Through all the country of the hills,
Among the vales and laughing rills,
All forms of life that breathed were slain,
In this most dark and fearful reign.[2]

On details here I need not dwell,
For pen can never trace nor tell
The thoughts that in my bosom swell:

[1] Josh. x. 12-14.—[2] x. 28-43.

I can not paint their deeds in rhyme,
No more than measure space and time.
And yet they seemed to serve the Lord,
Who blessed them with a great reward.
And gladly stayed the rolling sun,
To see their bloody work well done.

INTERLUDE.

(They knew not God, nor knew His law
That moves all worlds without a flaw:
They thought the earth on pillars stood,[1]
That ever held it firm and good;
But never seemed to think it best,
To tell on what the pillars rest.
They thought the sun that decks the sky,
In all his majesty on high,
Revolved in his appointed way,
Around the earth by night and day;
Ne'er dreaming that the sun stood still,
And earth revolved with matchless skill.
They thought the stellar worlds of light
That cheer the silent hours of night,
Were made in feeble light to burn,

[1] 1 Sam. ii. 8.

To serve our purpose in their turn.
They thought that God who rules above,
With truth and wisdom, peace and love,
Who hath but one revokeless aim,
Through all eternity the same,
Was but the servant of their race,
Who talked with Moses face to face,
And would defend his wayward seed,
And share with them each wicked deed.
Though dark *this* age, let joy awake,
That *some* have learned their sad mistake.)

———

Now Joshua, the son of Nun,[1]
Who did presume to hold the sun,
Could not revoke time's onward tide,
And at five-score and ten he died:
While Judah next, at God's command,
Was made the ruler of the land.[2]

May we not hope for better days?
That peace may shed her genial rays?
And deeds of love each soul employ,

[1] Josh xxv. 29.—[2] Jud. i. 2.

To light their future paths with joy?
But, lo! a dark and frowning page
Reveals a God yet full of rage,
Who pours the caldrons of His wrath,
And fills with death fair Canaan's path.
The early record of his reign,
Bears witness of ten thousand slain:
Of those not numbered with the dead,
Were seventy kings, who quickly fled;
But they were not allowed repose,
But were deprived of thumbs and toes,[1]
Which were cut off in their retreat,
And gathered up in piles of meat.
For all these deeds God was delighted,
And by Himself they were requited.[2]

With God's approval thus elated,
His bloody reign was not abated;
But quickly with his fiendish crew
He every soul at Zephath slew;[3]

[1] Jud. i. 4.—[2] i. 7.—[3] i. 17.

Then wound his way along the coast,[1]
With his infernal bloody host;
And Gaza, Ekron, Askelon,
Were rendered hopeless and forlorn.
They scaled the rugged mountain height,[2]
And chased the people in their flight;
The Lord was with them day by day,
To scatter death along their way.

When God and Judah reached the valley,
They found the people there to rally;
With iron chariots now at hand,
They made a bold successful stand,[3]
Defying all the Lord's command.
In deeds of death until this hour,
While seeming leagued with Satan's power,
No force or bars impede their way,
To check their passage night or day;
The rolling deep subdued his wrath,
And bared his bosom for their path;

[1] Jud. i. 18.—[2] i. 19.—[3] i. 19.

While Jordan's dark resistless tide,
Was in their pathway quickly dried,
And stood a wall on either side;
The sturdy walls of Jericho,
Were by the breath of priests laid low;
The golden orb that rules the day,
Was forced his journey to delay;
While sighs and groans of thousands slain,
Commingled in their onward train:
Thus *blind* success would seem to say,
All forces must their will obey.
But Satan, gorged with sin and blood,
Resolved to stay the swelling flood,
And by his tactics kindly planned,
To bless with peace the stricken land:
His schemes so clouded by disguise,
That God was taken by surprise.
Thus iron chariots now defied
All Israel's force and God beside.
And once again He is defeated,
Which had so often been repeated.

INTERLUDE.

(If they with God could not approach,
That ancient, iron, *one-horse coach*,
What could they do 'gainst Yankee lads,
With Parrott guns and iron-clads?)

By this defeat the contest was suspended,
All hope to rule the Canaanites seemed ended;
And Israel's tribes were left to choose their way,
To serve the Lord, or other gods obey.
Once free to act, they mingled with their foes,
While peace and concord soon dispelled their woes.
They left the God of battle and defeat,
That He might not His deeds of death repeat:
The battle-cry was hushed, no fierce alarm
Disturbed the day, no nightly foes to harm;
But peace now smiles with unmistaken love,
And joy awakes like joys that are above.[1]

[1] Judges i. 3–6.

They took each other's daughters and their sons,
And bound their union with their little ones;
A happy change delights each passing hour;
No angry God usurps vindictive power.
Who then can blame them in this happy day,
If *Israel's* God they chose to disobey?
A God who evil did Himself create;
Chose lying spirits in their dark estate,
To execute His base and dire control
Upon an unoffending harmless soul;
Thus giving license to the powers of evil,
And doing work that ought to shame the Devil.

Honest reader do not chide me,
For the Bible is beside me,
And I will transcribe with care,
Giving verse and chapter there.

The Lord was seated on His throne most high,

¹ 1 Kings, xxii. 19–22.

And all the heavenly hosts were passing by,
While thus unto the people He did call:
" Who will persuade Ahab that he may fall ?"
One and another in their way replied,
But one and all alike were each denied;
Until a lying spirit came and stood,
In vile audacity before the Lord,
Yet on the Lord such good impression made,
He put all other applicants in shade:
For *he* assured the Lord that he would *lie*,
And to His prophets would the truth deny:
The Lord delighted, said, "Thou wilt prevail,
Go forth with lying tongue thou shalt not fail! '

While thus the Lord was moved in the direction
Of having for a liar such affection,
He all His prophets' mouths at once did fill[1]
With lying spirits who obeyed His will.
God gave unholy statutes to deceive,

[1] Kings, xxii. 23.

And judgments under which they could not
   live.
And David, said to be of God's own heart,
As such in cruel deeds performed his part,
By forcing Ammon's children, without cause,
Beneath the teeth of harrows and of saws.[1]
Their reeking flesh next met the iron ax,
Then in the kilns of fire were burned like
   flax;[2]
All Ammon's cities shared this horrid fate,
Which pen can never paint nor tongue
   relate.
No line or word of censure can we trace,
In its connection, or in any place.
Thus David acted his ignoble part,
And proved himself "a man of God's own
   heart."[3]

Again I ask, Who, then can blame
   A nation bowed with grief,

---

[1] 2 Sam. xii. 31.— [2] 1 Chron. xx. 2, 3.— [3] Acts, xiii. 22.

For seeking gods of higher aim,
   To find with them relief,

Where peace might smooth their thorny path,
   And light some joyous way;
Where kindly words displacing wrath,
   Might cheer them day by day?

But sad their hopes, how quickly turned
   Their day to dismal night;
For Godly wrath yet hotly burned,
   With its vindictive might.

God sold them to their foes for slaves,[1]
   Where lingering hope might die;
Then tortured them to death's dark waves,
   And scorned their bitter cry.

Thus Abraham's "unnumbered" race,
   God's loved and chosen seed,

---

[1] Judges. ii. 14; x. 7.

To people every land and place,
    The ensign of His creed,

Are now abandoned to their fate,
    Nay more—to meet His wrath,
With maledictions of His hate,
    Converging in their path.

Thus God's great plan hath wholly failed,
    Which clearly is revealed;
His rival having e'er prevailed
    In each contested field.

Thus Satan, with unnumbered throng,
    Embracing tribes and nations,
God's former hope, His joy and song,
    Of many generations,

Are now within the Devil's clasp,
    Obedient to his will,
Who holds them all within his grasp,
    His purpose to fulfill.

And yet it seems a peaceful reign
  Would be the Devil's choice;
If undisturbed he could remain,
  And none oppose his voice;

For who can read that he hath waged
  A war on any nation?
Or even hath his *foes* outraged,
  In any generation?

But like a worthy, peaceful king,
  Whose throne seemed quite unshaken,
Devised the good and useful thing,
  To have the census taken.

King David yielded his command
  With cheerful resignation,
And freely gave his willing hand
  To Satan's wise vocation.

Thus David numbered Israel's seed—[1]

[1] 1 Chron. xxi. 1, 2; xxvii. 2.

This sore afflicted race,
By which he saw who were in need,
Or had no resting place.

An act that nations justify,
Where civil laws prevail,
Of which their records testify;
Then why should God bewail?

Though Satan took the census first,
Should envious hate pursue it?
Whate'er is *good*, should not be cursed,
No matter who may do it.

But David well performed his part,
While servant of the Devil;
And numbered all with cheerful heart,
Without apparent evil.

No doubt he loved his new employ,
For which he had great cause;

For righteous deeds bring peace and joy,
  Compared to kilns and saws

By which he murdered helpless man,
  Impelled by God's intent,
As part of His vindictive plan
  To torture and torment.

God's former host, and chosen seed,
  Were few and far between,
While those who were to take the lead,
  With open foes were seen.

Yet God to make his numbers great,[1]
  Called every man a hundred;
Which makes it plain why He should hate
  To have them rightly numbered.

For which He was so much displeased,
  His vengeance spoke again,

---

[1] 1 Chron. xxi. 3.

By blood would only be appeased,
  To flood the earth like rain.

Three forms of death from which to choose,[1]
  Laid David in great strait,
For he could only two refuse,
  Hence one must be his fate.

First, three years' famine in the land,
  With starving, ling'ring death;
Or die by foes with sword in hand,
  With three years' lease on breath;

Or three days' vengeance of the Lord,
  Throughout fair Israel's coast,
Or pestilence so wide and broad,
  Of which a fiend could boast.

He soon decides, though in a strait,[2]
  Within God's hands to fall;

[1] 1 Chron. xxi. 10.—[2] xxi. 13.

In hope that mercies very great,
  Might save himself and all.

But hope for mercy was in vain,[1]
  For pestilential ire
Baptizes seventy thousand slain,
  Fulfilling God's desire.

An angel next in God's command,
  Commissioned with His wrath,
Came down to desolate the land,
  And darken every path.

Jerusalem in all its pride,
  Was also doomed to fall;
Her streets to bear a crimson tide,
  And float a funeral pall.

But David now their cause did plead,[2]
  And said it was not they,

---

[1] 1 Chron. xxi. 14.—[2] xxi. 15–17.

Who counted Israel's wayward seed,
    Then why this people slay?

'Twas I who numbered Israel's race,
    Slay me, if any one;
Or strike my father's resting place,
    For justice should be done.

This little speech assuaged the Lord,
    Who now perceived His error,
His angel sheathed his thirsty sword,
    And calmed the raging terror.

Thus while the wailings of despair
    Were being hushed in death,
God's voice electrifies the air
    With warm repenting breath.

At once He gave the countermand,
    Revoking His decree,

[1] 1 Chron. xxi. 15.

"It is enough, stay now thy hand,
   And set the remnant free."

Thus God miscounts, decrees, abates,
   Repents of maddened rage,
And clusters these conflicting traits,
   On one recorded page.

INTERLUDE.

(O God of love—the Father of the race,
Whose kindly care pervades all time and space,
Whose will is law, through all extent the same,
Whose law is changeless as Thy holy name;
Whose throne and central point is everywhere;
Who giveth unto each Thy constant care;
Teach us to know, and love Thee as Thou art;
That Thou canst not from laws ordained depart;
That plans matured ere time's old march began,
Are yet the same unchanged and changeless plan
That worlds and systems in their wondrous rounds,
Have their rotation, circuit, laws, and bounds;
That every soul is molded by Thy hand;
Its being, end, and aim by Thee was planned;

That all alike are agents of Thy will,
Thy grand design and noble end fulfill.
We love, O God! to venerate Thy name,
But feel that Moses' God is not the same,
Or if the same, wert then misunderstood
By those who were considered wise and good.

It seems that every creed or tribe of earth,
Conceives a god, and gives Him form and birth,
Possessing all the traits of every tribe;
Thus while portraying God, *themselves,* describe;
And as they each advance in reason's light,
And have more just conceptions of the right,
A god of like improvement then appears,
Reflecting still their passions, loves, and fears;
Then let us turn from that benighted age,
When God, a jealous God, was fired with rage;
And may diviner wisdom from above,
Expand our souls to see a God of love.)

But progress ever marks each day and age,
And sheds some light on Israel's darkened page.
Thus Jeremiah in his *best* estate,[1]

[1] Jer. ii.

Saw God divested of His wrath and hate;
Who with a kind, expostulating air,
Now pleads for Israel with a Father's care;
And for a season uses moral suasion
To reinstate His wayward Jewish nation.
But knowing Him so well, so long of old,
They could with little grace His plea behold;
And chose to lead a less eventful life,
Free from oppression and the field of strife.

Their non-compliance with the Lord's request
Awoke the slumb'ring anger in His breast,
And like a lion from a sweet repose.
With fresh vehemence, grapples with His foes.
The very thunderbolts of heaven are hurled,
To scourge the face of a defenseless world;
The elements of vengeance, death and hate
(A fearful compound in the aggregate),
Swept man and beast and every thing around,
Including trees, and fruit upon the ground.[1]

[1] Jer. vii. 10.

The voice of gladness and the voice of mirth,
No longer mingled round the social hearth;
The bride and bridegroom mutely shared the fate
Of lands and cities, all made desolate:[1]
To strangers' arms their wives did God condemn,
And fields to others to inherit them.[2]

Ezekiel next takes up the sad refrain,
While peace and love evoke their gentle reign;
But God resolved with sword of death in hand,
To cut the good and bad from off the land;
That every soul may know that He, the Lord,
Will not unto its sheath return the sword;[3]
His indignation on them all will pour,
And blow His heated wrath from shore to
    shore.[4]
All left of Israel's house He counts as dross;
Hence to consume them all will be no loss;[5]
And as they gather silver, brass, and tin,
And with a furnace melt it deep within,

[1] Jer. vii. 34.—[2] viii. 7.—[3] Ezek. xxi. 3-5.—[4] xxi. 31.—[5] xxii. 18.

So will He gather them with vengeance dire,
And blast them with unceasing flaming fire;
And when these elements of death are felt,
He then will leave them in the flames to melt,
That they may know that He, the Lord, doth pour
His fury on them as in days of yore.[1]

Fair Zidon next shall bathe in human blood,
That He, the Lord, may *there* be understood.[2]

The land of Egypt shall be desolate,
And share with others His vindictive hate:
God with a net, will circle them around,
Then leave them all to die upon the ground,
The fowls of heaven, and beasts of all the earth,
Of ev'ry climate, longitude, and birth,
Are all invited by His fiendish will,

[1] Ezek. xxii. 20-23.—[2] xxviii. 22, 23.

From piles of human flesh to eat their fill!
Who but a demon could this feast prepare—
Invite these guests to such a bill of fare,
And look with pleasure on such fell despair?

INTERLUDE.

(O poor, deluded, superstitious men,
If Satan does the like, do tell me when;
If God is falsely charged in this strange tale,
Then own the truth, that justice may prevail.
Why hug delusion, till its rotten core
Is seen, and felt, by all who dare explore?
Why not defend the truth, and shame the lie,
And vindicate the ways of God most high?)

Sun, moon, and stars refused to give their light,
And veiled their faces from the awful sight.
Throughout the country all that did remain,
Both man and beasts, were by their maker slain.

When I, the Lord, make Egypt desolate,
And scourge the land once full, with famine great,
When I shall smite all those that therein dwell,
(Of course He sends their wayward souls to hell),
Then will they know Me, as in former days,
For none but God this character displays.[1]

Next Gog and Magog must His vengeance share,
And writhe in cruel death and dark despair:
Without tribunal or assigning cause,
God forces iron hooks into their jaws;
Then follow deeds that demons should despise,
To sanctify His name before their eyes.
Oh, who can estimate the blood He shed,
When seven long months would scarce inter the dead!

[1] Ezek. xxxii. 3-15.

"Thus will His holy name be magnified,"
And by a nation's murder "sanctified,"
And boasts of being Israel's Holy One,
While by these deeds He makes Himself thus known;[1]
For by His fruits must God Himself be seen,
As all are judged from peasant to the queen.
But many heinous deeds I must pass o'er,
And leap stale quagmires filled with human gore.

INTERLUDE.

(O ye blind guides, pray tell me, if you can,
Where Satan ever sought the life of man?
Much less to torture with vindictive wrath,
And scatter death through every winding path.
But God of Moses whom you each defend,
As man's all-loving and eternal friend,
You all declare made earth a vale of tears

[1] Ezek. xxxviii, xxxix.

And filled each soul with dismal doubts and fears;
Hath doomed mankind to an eternal hell,
In writhing torment evermore to dwell;
That God in wrath will fan the fiery coals,
While age on age in long succession rolls.
Where nameless tortures never, never cease,
But through unending ages will increase.
And yet you say a Father, just and kind,
Controls the whole, and fashions every mind.
O thoughtless man! to reason's voice incline,
Discard the conflict with God's love divine;
And see for once through superstition's night,
That He who made the whole, made all things right;
That by His wisdom, power, and changeless will,
All nature moves His mission to fulfill!

But as the record stands, 'tis plain to see,
That Satan ever holds supremacy;
That all God's chosen ones of every birth,
By Him selected to replenish earth,
Prefer to leave the constant field of strife,
And seek a more congenial, peaceful life.
Thus God perceives through His long bloody school,

That force can never win, nor passion rule.
God now might well indulge in thoughts of grief,
And thus soliloquize and seek relief:—
"What sad forebodings now engulf My soul,
While Satan hath dominion o'er the whole.
This earth so fair in its primeval state,
Where thornless flow'rs would bloom and vegetate,
Where fadeless verdure decked a brierless sod,
And man in his perfection equaled God,
Is all reversed, while sad and bitter years
Have made the world a wilderness of tears.
Must earth be wrested from My fond embrace,
And Satan rule and ruin all the race?
If so, then other worlds that float in space
May be the victims of his foul embrace:
And vast creation in its wondrous whole,
May yet be subject to his dire control.
From what is past, the worst I may expect;
On seas of blood my fondest hopes are wrecked.
My aching bosom swells with burdened sighs,
While hope, once buoyant, dwindles, fades, and dies.
O Earth! O Heaven! Is there no friendly
    power
To give Me hope in this most hopeless hour!
Are none in sadness left to weep, or tell
That Satan rules the whole, and peoples Hell!

O Vengeance! raise thy hand, renew the strife,
And probe the earth with thy relentless knife!"

But now a voice of love, from soul serene,
In gentle accents mingles in the scene,
And spake:—"My Father, spare, and in their stead
Let retribution fall upon my head:
I'll take upon Myself the form of man,
And vindicate Thy primal, faultless plan:
With kindly words and many loving deeds,
I'll fain adapt My life to all their needs;
With love for love, ay, love for those who hate,
I'll raise mankind to their primeval state.
All causes but produce their like effects,
As he who soweth seed the same expects;
Hate comes of hate, while anger feeds its fire;
While love for hate will banish hate's desire.
And, O My Father! I will be to earth,
A man of sorrow and of humble birth,
The lowly walks of human life I'll share,
And burdens of the poor and needy bear.
Their wayward footsteps ever will attend,
And be their true, confiding, faithful friend.
Thus will I hope their favor to command,
And fit them for a place at Thy right hand."

"My Son, Thy precepts all are new,

And yet they may be good and true;
But recompensing love for hate,
My honor thus to vindicate,
Is but rewarding evil deeds;
And yet You say it soweth seeds,
That will come forth in after days,
And mend their wicked, winding ways.
This strange philosophy, I own,
In all My teachings is not known.
But as My plans and powers have failed,
And sin and Satan have prevailed,
I'll waive My prejudice, and see
What good or ill May follow Thee;
I'll give My scepter to Thy hand,
And yield to Thee supreme command.")

In the fullness of time, or ripening of years,[1]
God's only begotten from Heaven appears,
In manger was born, where the cattle were
    fed,[2]
On hay for a pillow He first laid His head.
His advent thus humble, mid sorrows and
    tears,

[1] Gal. iv. 4.—[2] Luke ii. 7.

Foreshadowed the future of life's coming years:
The days of His childhood and youth were concealed,
But once until manhood His life is revealed;[1]
At length He, no longer obscure or disguised,
Is by John in the river of Jordan baptized:[2]
When, lo! the glad Heavens were opened above,
The Spirit descended in form of a dove;
A voice from the arches resounded, "My Son,
Thou art My beloved, for well hast Thou done!"

The Spirit from Heaven, with kindness sincere,
To Jesus, the Son of Jehovah, drew near,
And now introduced Him to Satan of old,
That He the great captain of earth might behold.
They cordially met, and together they walked,
To the top of a mountain they journeyed and talked,
Where Satan portrayeth the beauties of earth,

---

[1] Luke ii. 41–52.—[2] Mat. iii. 13–17.

The kingdoms he conquered, and what he was worth;
And said, "All these riches are now in Thy power,
If Thou wilt but serve me from this very hour."
But Jesus, revealing His force in reserve,
Said "Get thee behind me! God only I serve."
Satan then left Him not further entreating,
With seeming defeat in this their first meeting.[1]

This great moral conquest gave hope to the nations,
While angels greet Jesus with kind ministrations.[2]
His mission so holy, I need not relate,
How blessings met cursings and love followed hate.
That He healed the infirm, gave sight to the blind;

[1] Mat. iv. 1-10.—[2] iv. 11.

When falsely accused, no less loving and kind
How enemies scorned Him, derided and railed,
And many who loved Him, when needed most, failed.
But such was His life in its meekness and worth,
It seemed to surpass all examples of earth.
The good seed thus scattered by love's willing hand,
Seemed fruitful to bless and encompass the land;
And in its rich harvest abundance to yield,
While nations were reapers, this planet one field.
But sad the result, as the record appears,
The seed sown in love and thus watered with tears,
Was plucked from earth's bosom before it gave birth,
By Satan who sought the dominion of earth.
Thus thwarted the purpose of Father and Son,

For what he destroyed was a hundred to one.[1]

The contest waxed stronger, while day unto day,
The foes of Jehovah bore conquering sway;
And all the apostles with Christ were assailed,
While chief priests, in league with the Devil,
    prevailed.
Though great were the efforts of Father and Son,
The conquest by Satan seemed easily won.
Christ's wicked accusers were God's chosen seed,
Still led by the Devil, performed the dark deed.
And Judas was ready at Satan's command,
For thirty small pieces of silver in hand,
With a kiss to betray, and place Him in
    power
Of those who now sought Him, His life to
    devour.[2]

The Saviour then prayed in the sadness of
    grief,

[1] Mark, iv. 15.—[2] Mat. xxvi. 15, 16, 48.

That aid from His Father would give Him
   relief;
"Oh! if it be possible this cup to shun;
But Thy will, not Mine, O My Father! be done.[1]
My God, wilt Thou leave Me to die in their
   power?
Why hast Thou forsaken Me in this dark
   hour?"[2]
Thus Jesus in sorrow and anguish did pray,
That death and its terrors might all pass away.
But prayerful entreaties and efforts all failed,
While Satan emboldened in triumph prevailed.
Thus Jesus was taken to Pilate and tried,
Who doomed Him to hang on the cross till
   He died.

The sun veiled his face and withheld his warm
   light,[3]
Refusing to watch o'er the heart-rending sight:

---

[1] Mat. xxvi. 39.—[2] xxvii. 46.—[3] xxvii. 51.

The rock ribs of earth from their sockets were rent,
And the dead from their graves in earth's struggles were sent.
But Satan, triumphant, rejoiced in the gloom,
As Jesus was laid in the depths of the tomb.
Thus in the great contest with Father and Son,
The Devil was victor, though sadly he won.
From Eden's fair bowers, unto Calvary's height,
He has thwarted God's plans, and has won every fight;
And his broad, crooked road is still thronged every day,
While but few ever walk in the straight, narrow way.[1]

I would not pluck a gem from Jesus' brow,
Before whose name all monarchs well may bow:
But thus to deify that blessed name,
And think all others ought to do the same,
Is what he never claimed, much less did plan,

[1] Mat. vii. 13–14.

For he but called himself the son of man.[1]
Nor was he void of worldly care and strife,
Or wholly free from some mistakes in life.
Behold him, as he hungered by the way,
And saw a fig-tree, in the light of day;
While yet the time of figs was out of season,
To look for them did not accord with reason;[2]
And still he thought its fruit all ripe and fair,
Upon the leafy boughs were hanging there;
But to his disappointment none were found
Among the verdant leaves nor on the ground.
This so disturbed that calm and peaceful mind,
He to the great mistake was not resigned,
And therefore caused the tree to fade and die,
For thus deceiving him, while passing by.[3]

Could Christ be God, who knowing all, not know
The time and season when the figs should grow?

[1] He is called the Son of Man, by Himself and others, eighty times in the New Testament.
[2] Mark, xi. 13.—[3] Mat. xxi. 19.

And also seeing all, could he not see
If figs were there or not upon the tree?
And finding none, could God thus vent His
    spite,
And kill a harmless, senseless tree outright?
Is this the God who mapped the vault of space
With rolling worlds that keep their time and
    place?
Who marks the bounds of each revolving
    sphere,
While ages pass, and cycles disappear?
Yet counts the moments as they swiftly play,
And keeps the record of each passing day.

If he were God, no other will could harm,
None could betray, or signal death's alarm:
No supplication to a higher power,
Could swell his soul when threat'ning tempests
    lower;
And yet he prayed to God in earnest tone,

And said *Thy* will, O God, not *mine*, be done.[1]

But it is claimed his miracles combine
To prove that he, in truth, was the Divine.
Yet Christ doth say in language plain and true,
That greater deeds than mine shall others do.
"I can do nothing of myself alone;"[2]
Thus in God's strength I work, and not my own;
And though my second coming is revealed,
Yet God from me hath kept the time concealed."[3]
Christ also asserted which none can deny,
"I go to my Father, who's greater than I,"[4]
And whenever called good the statement denied,
And said, "*God* is good, and *none* other beside."[5]

Then do not call him God, while all can scan
Page after page that proves him but a man;

[1] Luke, xxii. 42.—[2] John, v. 30.—[3] Mat. xxiv 36.—[4] John. xiv 28.—[5] Mat. xix. 17; x. 18; Luke, xviii. 19.

But rather call him by his chosen name,
The " son of man," who sought no higher aim;
Yet let us seek in all that's good and great,
His noble life of love to imitate.
And though he was a man of favored birth,
A moral light-house in this darkened earth,
Yet not unlike all other men was born,
Who grope in darkness, or the earth adorn;
Which is the path that angels all have trod,
While they with Christ and us are SONS OF GOD.

O mortals! mark the folly of your creeds,
How they ignore a life of honest deeds,
And force belief in Christ as God of all,
Or be forever damned for Adam's fall.
Though deeds of love are daily our delight,
Though we despise the wrong and love the
    right,
The poor and needy may our bounty share,
In deeds that speak the language of true
    prayer,

'Twill not release the soul from endless hell,
Where angry God and demons ever dwell.[1]
But once believe, and bow the bended knee,
And Heaven is ours through all eternity,[2]
Though steeped in sin, or dyed in human blood,
Or make our path of life a crimson flood,
Belief in Christ will make us white as wool,
And give us fellowship with God in full.[3]

Will this suffice, is asked with wild delight,
To change a demon to angelic light?
The church declares there is no other way,
And then will qualify their creeds, and say:
You must believe that Christ and God are one;
That Christ is God, and yet God's only son;
That Satan thwarted God when Adam fell,
And doomed the race of man to endless hell;
That God in grief repented making man,
Because the Devil foiled Him in His plan.[4]

[1] Psalm vii. 11; cxxxix. 8.—[2] Mark, xvi. 16.—[3] Isa. i. 18.—Gen. vi. 6.

That His designs with man have ever failed;
That sin and Satan ever have prevailed;
That when God came to earth in its dark hour,
To rescue man from Satan's ruling power,
In this great contest God Himself was slain,
And all His efforts to escape were vain.[1]
They only took His mortal life, you say,
While His divine survived the dreadful day;
But I in kindness will the creeds implore,
To tell if any ever murdered more.

You must believe that Satan's scheme devised
That God should be rejected and despised,
And that the masses should His name deny,
And by His chosen race was doomed to die.
That those selected as the only seed,
To represent His name in word and deed,
Led on by Satan's will, performed the crime
And cast the shadow on the face of time.
That Nature mourned without a God, in gloom,

[1] Mat. xxvi. 36-44.

Until He burst the bars that bound the tomb.

You must believe that men are all depraved,[1]
And that but few of all mankind are saved;[2]
Yet by God's cruel death, oh, strange to tell,
These few are thus released from endless hell;
For every creed declares all hope is vain,
If Christ the son of God had not been slain;
And yet I think no creed will dare deny
That Satan caused the Lord their God to die:
Thus it would seem that all who rest in peace,
May thank the Devil for their kind release!

You must believe that Christ's great trump will sound,
And waken all that sleep beneath the ground;
That bone to bone, with bodies, limbs, and veins,

---

[1] Psa. liii. 1, 3 ; Rom. iii. 12.—[2] Mat. xx. 16.—[3] Acts, xx. 28 Rom. v. 9, &c., &c.—[4] 1 Cor. xv. 52-54.

Will be replete with their old nerves and
    brains:
That every soul of Adam's ancient race,
Are held in doubt, in some sequestered place,
Are waiting for the last great judgment day,
While mournful years and ages pass away;
But strange to tell, this trumpet's awful blast,
Will bring their soulless bodies forth at last,
And, as the Judge decides, in Heaven or Hell,
Both soul and body must forever dwell;
That while eternal ages wend their way,
All must be cumbered with this load of clay;
And that the sober few with waving palms,
Will ever praise God's name by singing
    psalms.[1]

All this you must believe, and more,
If you would reach *their* heavenly shore.

Who can believe what seemeth but a lie?
But if I could, I'd rather starve and die,

---

[1] Rev. vii. 9.

Than stifle reason and all sense of right,
To blind my eyes, and swear there is no light!
Belief is the persuasion of a soul,
Which force of circumstances *must* control.
No wonder that "not many wise obey,"
Or "travel on the straight and narrow way,"[1]
Or that the broad and crooked thoroughfare,
Is thronged with men of sense who travel there.
For those who dare to walk by reason's light,
Prefer the day to superstition's night;
And thus obey the laws of God within;
All doing less, must live in conscious sin;
None can do more, for God in His behest,
But governs all as seemeth wise and best.
Thus should all souls their highest thoughts obey—
Be finite gods in all they do and say.

O Reason, lend thy hand, let truth prevail,
Before whose light all dismal creeds must fail!

[1] 1 Cor. i. 26.

And may a God of Holy Love be known,
A God who rules creation as His own,
Without a power to hinder or delay,
While nature moves in its appointed way:
A God with but one plan, one grand design,
In which all systems, suns, and spheres com-
    bine;
While man, the crowning apex of the whole,
Like suns and worlds is subject to control.
And yet in man all forms and powers combine
A union of the human and divine,
The ultimatum of God's grand design.
And as the spheres revolve their tireless rounds
Man still progressing hath no spheres nor bounds;
But while unending ages onward roll,
No power will check the progress of a soul.

THE VOICE OF PRAYER.

PRELUDE.

THE aspirations of the soul ascend
On wings of hope, to scenes divinely fair;
Nor bars nor bolts can hold the silent power
That seeks the elements of light and love !
Then cherish every longing of the soul.
Let thoughtful prayer dispel all slavish fear,
Let radiant hope extend her full-fledged wings;
For all our prayers and hopes, but dimly paint
The lofty heights to which we will attain.

THE VOICE OF PRAYER.

True prayer is a boon to the sorrowing soul,
The anchor of hope when the dark billows roll;
The magnet that points through the gloom to the star,
And guides our frail bark to the haven afar.
It opens within every channel of love,
And brings us in union with angels above—
'Tis a ladder that lifts every child of the sod
In closer communion with Nature and God.
It strengthens the soul in its hallowed powers,
To merit the land with its evergreen bowers;
It lightens the burdens of sorrow and gloom,
And cheers the dark passage that arches the tomb.
Yet our prayers *must* accord with *immutable laws*,
Else we pray for effects *independent of cause*.

But the zealot declares, "If in *faith* you implore,
All prayers will be answered in bountiful store;

Though faith may but equal a small mustard
    seed,
To the sin stricken soul it supplies every need,
While even the mountains will heed his decree,
And leap with one bound to the depth of the
    sea!" *

But who can have faith that ignores every sense?
The very assumption is empty pretense,
And rivets the chains to a cowardly slave,
Divested of all that is noble and brave;
Whose faltering tongue can but feebly express
What manhood and honor would gladly suppress;
Whose faithless petitions oft burden the air,
Directing his Maker through long, windy prayer,
Where the line of His duties explicitly run,
Their order and details when all should be
    done;

* Mat. XXI, 21.

Whose vain innuendoes, if answered at all,
The rounds of creation would stagnate and fall!
Oh man! *be* a man in the sense of a soul
Full conscious of faith in a Father's control,
A faith that unlocks the deep caverns of thought,
Regardless of phantoms that bigots have wrought.
A faith that illumines the vault of the skies,
Where joys are eternal—where hope never dies,
Where every immortal with boundless desires,
In its zenith of glory will kindle new fires!
For scenes so transporting, to shorten the way,
Let faith ever move us to labor and pray.

Ever pray *with the law*, so shall harmony reign,
And your prayers will not mock you, as utterly vain.

Then pray that the shadows may fall from your
    eyes,
That truth may but triumph, while prejudice
    dies,
That all may embrace what their highest
    thoughts crave,
Each think for himself, not be led like a slave;
That reason and conscience may ever prevail,
Though cherished opinions forever may fail;
Then fervently pray in the light of God's
    laws,
That prayers may be heard, as *effects* follow
    cause.

But to pray that the Lord will in mercy come
    down,
To feed some poor beggar that comes to your
    town,
Is asking your Maker in kindness to do
Precisely the work He has given to you.

How vain are the prayers that the starving be fed,
Compared to bestowing a morsel of bread.

To pray that kind showers may in bounty descend,
That earthquakes and hurricanes ne'er may offend—
That fire may not burn you, and water not drown—
To jump from a steeple and gently come down,—
Is asking Jehovah to alter His law,
As much as to say you've detected a flaw!

To pray that the innocent suffer for crime,
That we in our folly committed through time,
Is to censure the passage that all should revere,
Which saith, that "the guilty can *never go clear:*" *

* Ex. xxxiv. 7.

No repentance, no *faith* can e'er banish a woe,
For the truth is revealed, "*all must reap what they sow.*" *

No *forgiveness* can ever change tares into wheat,
He who sows, must *uproot* them, and learn by defeat;
Then blend all your prayers with this *true* revelation,
That "each for *himself must* work out his salvation"! †

We must grow from within or in weakness must fall,
To trust to another, we jeopardize all,
Our wills must arouse us to labor and pray,
And hold us to duty's benificent way.
This school of self culture will lead us at length
To rely on our powers, and to grow in our strength;

* Gal. vi. 7. † Phil. ii. 12.

Thus upward and onward from earth to the skies,
We'll work our own passage by working to rise

The "Prodigal Son" in the annals of time,
Gives blessings unearned to a dark life of crime;
Behold him estranged from the home of his youth—
A wayward apostate to virtue and truth,
Exhausting his substance by riotous strife,
He beggars himself in the morning of life;
He poisons the stream from the fountain divine,
Till at last he becomes but a servant of swine!
The fruit of his folly he feels to despise,
To return to his father he now doth arise;
But what a transition awaiteth his name,
And what a reward for his folly and shame!
From swine in their filth and from penniless woe,
He flies like an arrow that's sped from a bow,
And alights where the tumults of gladness await,

Where he's feasted and clad in the fashion of
 state;
Embellished in garments of princely attire,
Of all others he now is the one to admire.
His brother who never had swerved from the
 right,
Was veiled in the shadows of his brilliant light;
No wonder he felt that injustice and wrong,
Was feasting the wayward—was breathed in
 their song.
Even the prodigal on his return,
Manfully chose like a servant to earn
His way to promotion, by labor and care,
Till justice awarded a portion his share.
And this is the law by which all must arise,
From the shadows of earth to the light of the
 skies.

A rapid transition from sinner to saint,
An artist may fashion with canvass and paint;

But *Nature* unfoldeth her germs by degrees,
From the tiniest flower to the sturdiest trees;
And man in his progress this law must fulfill,
Whose life currents swell by the force of his will.
Then let us all pray that our work be well done,
And avoid the broad road of the prodigal son;
And may all awards and all blessings be spurned,
Not founded in justice—not honestly earned.

The oak all alone on the top of the hill,
   With roots that lay hold of the rocks,
Defieth the storm with a confident thrill,
   The earth with its heavings and shocks.

But to grow in the valley surrounded by trees,
   Where each gives protection to all,
Where tornadoes in fragments come soft as a breeze,
   Divided, they totter and fall.

Then let us in weakness develop to strength—
  Grow strong like the oak on the hill,
For patient endurance will conquer at length,
  By the force of invincible will.

To fully possess we must honestly earn,
  All else will be counted as naught;
By self application we only can learn,
  Or scale the bright summit of thought.

Then ever be grateful for something to do,
  And *do it* with cheerful good will,
Defying all evil be noble and true,
  And grow like the oak on the hill.

But total depravity's withering blight,
Still mantles the church in a sorrowful night,

And creeds in their darkness as ever distrust
Man's reason as carnal, his virtues but lust;
Disclaiming all merit in duty well done,
They lean on the arm of God's dutiful son;
In weakness and darkness they plod the same
    rounds,
Discarding the wisdom of changing their bounds,
All moral achievements of whatever name,
And deeds of a demon are counted the same,
So far as the *merits* of either *avail*,
As *neither* can weigh in an orthodox scale.

But *Calvin's* adherents in *doctrine* maintain,
That *even* the merits of *Christ* are all vain;
That foreordination defines the elect,
And limits all reprobates God will reject;
Transgression can forfeit no claim to the throne,
No virtue can ever rob hell of its own!
In this sad dilemma we never can tell,

Which is our destiny, heaven or hell!
So each bides his time, and ever must wait,
Till the judge in all kindness announces our
    fate!
Oh what a delusion for men to believe!
What teachers, when teaching is but to deceive!
What a license to indolence, folly and crime,
To darken the sands in the pathway of time!
Oh reason and justice illumine the way,
And be their companions whenever they pray.

Man prays that his Maker would lengthen his
    days,
While the laws of his being he seldoms obeys;
The spirit immortal will gladly depart
When life-giving fountains congeal at the heart;
No law is suspended should earth everywhere
Unite in one chorus, to swell the same prayer!

An honest old negro most ardent in prayer,
With reason and faith not developed with
    care,
In asking God's blessing on each frugal meal,
For what he most needed made earnest ap-
    peal.
A wag who perceived his potatoes were gone,
With basket brim full, at the earliest dawn,
Secreted himself in the cabin o'er head,
Where the negro below him yet slumbered in
    bed;
Who soon roused to cooking the best he was
    able,
And under the hatchway spread out his pine ta-
    ble.
Without a potatoe to grace any plate,
He seated himself, yet bewailing his fate,
Exclaimed, "O my Fader, in merciful love,
Give Cuffy some 'taters from bounties above."
At once the potatoes came showering down,
Upsetting his dishes, and pelting his crown!

"O them's um, them's um, bless de Lord, O
    my soul!
Who cares for de coffee, de pitcher and bowl?
De shower of big 'taters, O Lord, am sub-
    lime,—
But I pray dat you leff um down easy next
    time."

Whether fiction or fact, this illustrates, I
    deem,
That *some* answers to prayer are not *all* that
    they seem.

Then pray that your prayers with God's laws
    ever blend
In union with *deeds*, that will bless and ex-
    tend;
For these are the prayers that the Lord ever
    heeds,
Regardless of color, of birth, or of creeds.

Our homes that protect us from sunshine and storm,
Are prayerful emotions in tangible form:
Asylums and churches, and schools everywhere,
Are fruits of our labor commingled with prayer.
Admitting their errors, I pity the thought
That chides every movement not perfectly wrought,
For each hath a mission, and laudable plan.
And rather than censure, improve, if you can:
Fraternal forbearance, and charity should
Excuse many follies, where *motives* are good.

The church all advise us that Christ taught with care,
Not only the duty, but *manner* of prayer,
Yet his prayers were in private—alone he retired,
Where his thoughts undiverted to heaven aspired;

In the depth of the forest at evening's repose,
When Nature forgets all her turmoil and woes,
There Christ wends his way, from the scenes of commotion,
And his altar illumes with the flames of devotion! *
By example and precept he taught evermore,
To enter our closet, and shutting the door
In secret to pray: and that moments thus spent,
Would surely reward us wherever we went.†
But to pray before men at the corners of streets,
Or with multitudes thronging the synagogue's seats,
Is to be like the hypocrites, selfish and vain,
Who thus seek the praises of men to attain.‡

* Mat. xiv. 23, Mark vi. 46, Luke v. 16, also vi. 12.
† Mat. vi. 6.   ‡ vi. 5.

Then enter your closet—*your soul's center
    closet*,
Alone with your God, with your thoughts deep
    within,
There pray that you ever, by earnest endeavor,
May fight the good fight and the victory win.

A word kindly spoken the right time and place,
May lift some dark soul from the depths of
    disgrace;
May waken a prayer on the altar of love,
That ends in fruition, with angels above:
We thus build a ladder,—each deed is a
    round,—
That reaches to heaven, while touching the
    ground;
For in aiding the least is involved the reward—
' Enter thou into the joy of thy Lord." *

* Mat. xxv. 31, 23.

Then pray with your purse, with kind words
and good deeds;
O pray that our churches may think less of
creeds,
That ever the poor may be welcomed within,
Though garments are tattered—souls blotted
with sin—
And that love, pure, unselfish, each heart may
expand,
And peace, with its blessings pervade every
land.

O pray that intemperance wither and die,
That man, disenthralled, set his mark ever
high;
That Nature may never indict us for treason,
That man slake his thirst at the fountain of
reason.
That the sword may succumb to the power of
the pen,
And be sheathed by the highest tribunals of
men.

O pray for the children that beg by the way,
So friendless, no kindness to cheer the long day;
Their minds while yet tender by love are impressed,
Then plant your affections within their young breast;
Who knows by the surface the treasures below?
Where grateful emotions their forces bestow?
You may haply develop a germ in the soul,
That will from that moment have strength of control.
Then nurture the children—the dear loving children,
That smilingly greet us wherever we turn,
Instruct them to triumph, that bearing life's burden,
Its lessons of patience and power they may learn.

May woman (God bless her!) have equal position
With man, under law, and in *every* condition.
Her "ballot" so gentle like "snowflakes" descending—
With feminine features through laws interblending,
May round the rough angles of turbulent man,
That she in her genius *may be all she can.*
Her true intuitions, oft valued as naught,
Will reach a conclusion with flash of a thought;
While man with his reason, though massive and strong,
With pond'rous assumptions comes plodding along!

Remember the Indians with filial affection,
And give them our laws, with their arms of protection.
O pray for yourself in the depth of your soul—
That passion and appetite never control—
That wisdom may guide every action of life—
That love conquer hatred, and banish all strife.

If a husband, or wife, then nurture with care
Reciprocal love, from the fountain of prayer;
Your little attentions should daily entwine,
Like tendrils that hold every fast-clinging vine.

Your children should walk in the breath of your love,
While teaching earth's lessons, direct them above.
O make your homes happy with cheerful delight,
And children like *chickens* will come home at night;
And none of your household will willingly roam,
But ever remember "*There's no place like home.*"

It was labor with prayer that dotted the seas
With the sails of the mariner filled by the breeze,

And gave him the compass which points to the
   star,
To guide him in safety o'er oceans afar.

The prayer of Columbus 'mid slander and
   wrong,
Gave birth to Columbia's beautiful song.
How sadly he prayed, 'till his labors were
   blest,
With a home for the world "In the Land of
   The West."
Then labor and pray 'till the isles of the sea,
Inscribe on their banner "THE LAND OF THE
   FREE"!

We little know by what enduring strife,
Our fathers brought this continent to life;
How long and weary were their early years,
How sad and dreary were their daily fears,

While untaught Nature frowned at every blow,
And like the red man was their stalwart
    foe;
How Britain ever claimed the "Lion's share"
Of their unceasing toil and anxious care,
And yet they bore oppression like a sage,
Until endurance kindled into rage,
Then they proclaimed, "henceforth *we will be
    free!*"
And sank old Britain's taxes with her tea.
Then came their seven years' war—a seven fold
    strand,
That bound their hearts in one heroic band;
One prayer was borne on their united breath,
"O give us Liberty, or give us death!"
At last triumphant they became a Nation,
And States were Stars of one Grand Constella-
    tion!

   But early in their weary toil,
   In felling trees to till the soil,

Their brawny arms though hard and strong,
By toiling early, late and long
Their hearts though brave and ever true,
To build this Western World anew,
Were feeble in their force and skill,
Compared to their *unbending will;*
Their *needs* were father of this prayer,
That burst upon the willing air:

"Aid, for the toiler in his strife!
Aid, for a Nation's early life!
Aid, for our wives who spin and weave!
Their toilsome hours we pray relieve!
Aid, that our lands may not repose,
But bloom in beauty like the rose.
Let forests bow their stately pride,
That we may o'er their ashes ride;
Let Towns, and Cities rear their heads,
For those who sleep in *trundle beds:*
Come! any force, whate'er it be,
And we will join our fate with thee."

Their prayers were heard o'er hill and
    plain,
Nor did they supplicate in vain:
For laughing streams, whose voices rang,
As down the cliffs they danced and sang,
Were checked amid their mirthful reel,
And made to turn a water-wheel!

Then steam that hissed with foaming pride,
Defying all the powers beside,
Was caught within an iron cage,
While boiling o'er with heated rage!
His force excited naught could hold,
And though his will was scarce controlled,
It was observed, if not abused,
His forces could be wisely used.
Then spindles hummed at his behest—
O'er ocean towered his cloudy crest.
The iron horse the wind outran,
And made the world anew for man!

The lightning from the clouds was caught—
And vitalized with living thought;
Our Franklin reined the flaming steed,
While Morse subdued him to our need,
Whose heart propels˙ electric fires,
Around the world on slender wires!

With magic life new scenes unfurled
Their wonders to a new-born world!
Our iron ribs across our breast,
Bore loaded wheels at our behest;
The reins of thought were in our hands,
While we conversed with distant lands;
Our fertile fields from shore to shore,
Fed other Nations from our store;
While every tongue, and tribe of earth,
Was welcomed at our Nation's hearth:
We grew in numbers, wealth and power,
And lived an age in every hour!

But pride the bane of worldly strength,
Grew with our growth until, at length,
A viper coiled around our heart,
And chilled our blood by fiendish art.
Thus stupefied we ceased to pray,
While his cold coils extended lay.
Until a mother's burdened prayer,
Electrified the midnight air:
With frenzied lamentations wild,
She prayed, "O give me back my child!
O God, return my darling boy,
And fill a mother's soul with joy!"

Her prayer was echoed far and wide,
It caught the breeze and kissed the tide,
Responses met her earnest plea
For Justice, Truth, and Liberty.
Yet all the powers of hell were hurled,
To choke the prayers that shook the world!

But Justice held her even scales,
In which the right at length prevails;
And though the blood of thousands slain
With iron hail, was shed like rain;
Though conflict raged most fierce and strong
Though days were dark and years-so-long,
Yet Freedom's glorious banner rose
Triumphant, over all our foes!

O hills, and dales, and laughing streams,
Kissed by the Sun's enamored beams,
Send your glad shout from sea to sea—
"*One Land on God's green Earth is free*"!

Free? Think, Oh man, in this glad hour
Doth *Woman* share thy freedom's dower?
Remember—God bestows His care
Of sex regardless everywhere—
All are the equal children—all,
Of Him who notes the "sparrow's fall."

Must she who is thy counterpart—
The sunny side of every heart—
The part essential to the whole,
Not have a voice in self-control?

Must woman in her high behest,
Obey alone what man thinks best,
And bow to his supreme control,
A thoughtless, helpless, prayerless soul?
Be taxed like man, like man obey,
Moulded by him like potter's clay?

Must he who wins a loving heart,
By his illusive, fiendish art,
Be not disgraced, though undisguised,
While *she is ruined, and despised?*

Must she who rears her noble sons—
Her daughters fair, from little ones,
Have naught to say what laws shall bless
A mother's love, and tenderness?

Shall legal murder scourge the land,
Whose poison dens at every hand
Are portals to a drunkard's grave,
And *woman have no power to save?*
O man invoke her loving aid,
That all these evils may be stayed.

The prayers of our fathers were more than they seemed,
When the sunshine of Liberty over them beamed,
For when they proclaimed equal rights throughout earth!
Our Goddess conceived, and ere long will give birth,
For her pain and her labor foreshadow the morn,
When Freedom the child of her love will be born.
Then laws will protect every child of the sod,
And know no distinction, like Nature and God.

Then man will in peace and in purity grow,
Without the intrusion of, Why do ye so?
Our honest convictions like sunbeams will greet,
And many-toned colors will blend as they meet;
Then all will be judged by the standard of worth,
Regardless of wealth or distinction of birth.
Our churches wide open, divested of creeds,
Will mould their instruction to man's highest needs:
Their lessons of wisdom will teach self-control—
A health-giving fountain to body and soul.
The gospel of love will with laws interblend,
In union with deeds, for a glorious end:
With one common brotherhood under the sun,
All union of interests center in one.
Our natures expanded by freedom of thought,
Though all become teachers, all seek to be taught;

Yet thought in its channel, like rivers will flow
To the Ocean of Truth, as still onward we go;
Till the Banner of Peace and Good Will is unfurled,
To all Oceans and Lands that encircle the World!
That all these rich blessings may bloom everywhere,
Let Nations unite in *effectual* Prayer.

Testimonials.

From the many critical notices and reviews of "THE VOICES" we have only room for a few brief extracts.

Judge BAKER of New York, in his elaborate review of "THE VOICES," says: "Considered in the light of a controversial or didactic poem, it is without an equal in contemporaneous literature—the birth of an audacious mind, and is destined to excite greater and more wide encircling waves of sectarian agitation than any anti-credal work ever published."

Prof. S. B. BRITTAN, in his able review of the work, says: "In the Voice of Nature the author gives us a clearer insight into his own views of the material world, of human nature and God. He has a rational philosophy of the relations of mind and matter, and his theology is at once natural and charitable. He recognizes one God everywhere, present alike in the physical world and in His moral universe. The God he adores, and his strong faith in the goodness that rules the world, are clearly revealed and forcibly expressed in the following paraphrastic and poetical rendering of a beautiful passage in the Sermon on the Mount:

> Will He who hears the ravens when they cry,
> Mock and deride thee when no hope is nigh?
> Will He who clothes the lilies of the field,
> That neither toil, nor spin, nor raiment yield;
> Who feeds the fowls that never reap nor sow—
> Extends His watchful care where'er they go:
> Will He who clothes the grass which is to-day,
> While all its beauty quickly fades away,
> Forget His image—His immortal child!
> Is he alone derided and defiled?
> Or left to tread the downward thoroughfare,
> With Satan to bewilder and ensnare,
> And urge him on to death and dark despair?
> "O, ye of little faith!" *let reason sway:*
> *Are not your souls more precious far than they?*

WILLIAM H. BURLEIGH, a well-known author and poet, in one of his contributions to the Chicago *Evening Post*, thus speaks of the author and "THE VOICES:" "That he is a bold, earnest man, with very pronounced opinions, that he has a combative and incisive way of stating those opinions, and that, below all seeming antagonism to the letter of old creeds, he accepts the spirit of the new dispensation, his book furnishes abundant evidence. His verse is generally characterized by vigor, and at times glides with a true rythmetic flow, and rings with a genuine poetic harmony."

www.ingramcontent.com/pod-product-compliance
Lightning Source LLC
Chambersburg PA
CBHW021838230426
43669CB00008B/1007